INTO WINE

An invitation to pleasure

Santé!!

Olivier Magny

INTO WINE

Copyright © 2013 Olivier Magny
All rights reserved – Gourmand Horizons,
New Orleans, LA (www.gourmandhorizons.com)
Cover Design by Marie Sourd
ISBN-10: 1482369451
ISBN-13: 978-1482369458 (Gourmand Horizons)

To A.

INTO WINE

TABLE OF CONTENTS

Foreword	p.6
Introduction	p.8
"Get a real job"	p.14
The road to pleasure and knowledge	p.18
Secrets of the soil	p.32
Gentleman farming	p.40
Terroir: the keystone to wine	p.54
Super grapes!	p.68
From winemaking to making wine	p.86
Labels decoded	p.106
Beating wine marketing	p.122
PR: Don't trust the hype	p.134
Tasting like a pro	p.148
Be a terroirist!	p.160
Postface	p. 174
Appendix	
25 wine FAQs	p. 177
Recommended wineries	p. 195
O Chateau, the rest of the story	p. 210
Special Offer	p. 218

INTO WINE

FOREWORD

Wine changed my life.

The ways I think, eat, drink and work have all been deeply transformed by my journey in wine. As a result, I am now happier, healthier and more optimistic.

By journey in wine, I'm not referring to the countless hours of jolly drunkenness, but instead to the enlightening learning adventure along the wine way.

This is the adventure I will share with you in the following pages: one that should help you not only gain a much better understanding of wine, but also grasp the beauty, and maybe the necessity of the inspiring *art-de-vivre* wine unveils for us.

And who knows, just like wine changed my life, it may change yours too.

INTO WINE

INTRODUCTION

"Jargon always masks ignorance." I was eighteen when one of my professors said that in class. At the time, I could not make sense of this statement. To me, jargon was the opposite of ignorance; it was about knowledge, and probably one of its most visible symptoms.

Only years later did I come to understand the true meaning of my professor's words. Being a sommelier, I've had the privilege to meet a few extraordinary people. Funny how brilliant people tend to use simple words. They leave fancy words to others. Their field of expertise suddenly becomes fascinating and approachable. They make you feel as if you too could write a symphony, explore the genome or create a great wine.

Wine's been my profession for over ten years now, and when I look back, I believe that what really pushed me to embrace this career was the wine jargon. I loved wine and I couldn't stand the way wine professionals talked about it. The words experts chose to talk about wine only erected the barriers they claimed to undo. Wine jargon to me was the negation of wine: the triumph of words over emotion. As a young wine lover, I figured it was my duty to go piss off a few French wine snobs.

So off I went.

But out of all the obscure nonsense infused in the world of wine, there is one word I'm in love with—one word the French language had the elegance to give birth to and to nurture. That word is: *terroir*.

Defining *terroir* is a recurring occupation for wine lovers. For many, *terroir* simply means the soil—the soil where the very vine was planted. This soil will define the style of your grapes, and consequently of your wine. Some prefer a broader definition[1]. Some even push it so far as to add a human dimension: those who grow the grapes and make the wine.

Brilliant wine writer Matt Kramer came up with what I find to be the best translation of the concept into English. His definition pays a poetic tribute to the cultural dimension of the concept: *terroir* is *"somewhereness"*.

When I teach a class, to explain what *terroir* is, I take two glasses of wines made with the same grape, coming from the same exact village[2], and have students taste them. Made with the same exact grape, from vineyards that are a few meters away from one another, the wines have a lot in common, yet are totally different. And whether students are professionals or novices, they all notice that difference.

---

[1] Adding subsoil structure and composition, microclimate, humidity, topography, exposure, etc.
[2] Two Sancerre, two Meursault, two Hermitage, etc.

What predominantly[3] separates the wine in those two glasses is *terroir*. *Terroir* is the possibility of authentic singularity.

Ask a wine lover what makes a great bottle of wine so great: *le terroir*. Why is this winemaker so excited about this small little parcel on that particular hill? *Le terroir*. What is so wonderful about Burgundy or Piemonte? *Le terroir*.

Le terroir is what turns wine lovers on.

It is the key to their pleasure. It plays with their intellect and with their taste buds. But leaving aside their tendency to snobbery, wine lovers are no different from other people. We *all* love our taste buds and our intellects to be tickled.

We all need *terroir*.

We need *terroir* in our glasses, on our plates, on our streets, and in our conversations. I believe that *terroir* is a path to happiness.

That is what this book is about. It is about building a deliberately bumpy and all the more delectable road to a happier life.

---

[3] Provided that I work with wines about which I know the winemaking, so that the winemaking process doesn't affect too dramatically the expression of *terroir* – more explanation in chapter 7.

INTO WINE

PART 1

How it all started...

INTO WINE

CHAPTER 1

"Get a real job!"

Choosing a career

Every single day, people ask me how I started to work in wine. My mom, on the other hand still weeps asking herself *why* I did so. When did she mess up? That's *her* question.

I was a good kid indeed – made good grades and all. Attended a good business school. She had every right to expect for me to become a respectable man, tie-wearing that is.

But I chose another path. While attending business school, I got to see first-hand the life high paying jobs led to, and I decided that life was not for me. So I tried to think of the life I would like to live. My main criterion at the time was not to contribute to making the world any uglier. Sounds silly and childish but let me tell you: it narrows down the list. Big time.

So wine I picked. Beautiful, endearing, tempting wine.

That's how it all started: a twenty something with idealistic thoughts.

Now, once I had made my decision, I realized that my business school degree (writing this, I realize how wonderfully relevant the initials of "business school" are) was going to be no help. *Au contraire*. I needed skills, knowledge and contacts and I had none. Zero.

So I rolled up my sleeves. Studied voraciously, tasted unreasonably, studied some more and studied again. After a few months, I started a company whose activity was to sell wine. It was called O Chateau. I hated it: going to random people's homes at night to try and sell them bottles was a little bit like hell to me. Working mostly at night, I needed to occupy my days. Since I dabbled with English, I decided to try and offer wine tasting sessions in English in the daytime. After a few weeks, I got my first clients for a two-hour session. It went on for five. I had a blast. On the metro ride home that night, I decided I would do that. O Chateau was born again. And this time, I was loving it.

Messy beginnings

> "Don't judge each day by the harvest you reap but by the seeds that you plant."
> — Robert Louis Stevenson

Saying that my beginnings in the wine world were messy is an understatement. I started O Chateau in my parents' Parisian apartment — which is no wine world epicenter. I was on my own, running my tastings from a couple of Parisian restaurants, between lunch and dinner services. My typical day involved going to the bakery, carrying my cases of wine and my baguettes with me on the metro, prepping my tasting, cleaning up my tasting and at the end of the day, doing the math and having made no money. Call me an overachiever.

After a few months, I decided to start offering tastings in an apartment of my own. I moved into a great loft that imaginatively enough I called "the wine loft" – remarkable trick to distract potential clients from the fact they would actually have to come to the hood to attend a wine tasting.

The area indeed was not picture perfect. Once they passed the gate, clients had to walk along a long dark alley surrounded with broken windows, only to reach a courtyard. The courtyard was not populated by the jovial Parisians tourists like to marvel at but instead by Chinese immigrants loading fabric and cheap clothes into beat up trucks. Once they spotted building D, clients entered what might have been one the ghettoest stairwells in Paris, with graffiti, suspicious smells, a perpetually broken freight elevator and four flights of stairs for them to climb up. By then, all the enthusiasm they had an hour before, when they left their hotel to attend what they probably imagined to be and elegant wine tasting session in Paris, was long gone. Most of them had switched into survival mode, mentally rehearsing their self-defense moves.

At the time, making it to "the wine loft" implied getting ready to be mugged[5].

Define "real".

At the time, my mom kept asking me to "get a real job" and stop this madness. But I didn't. And

---

[5] Along with being comfortable with walking through my bedroom to reach the restroom.

quite honestly, I'm not really sure why. For years, while most of my friends were enjoying a comfortable lifestyle, nice French-style paid vacations, I was beyond broke and never getting a day off. There were a lot of great moments but to say I was loving it would be a lie. The wine life at my level was not exactly glamorous. It implied a lot of convincing clients I was not a mugger, dishwashing, drying out glasses, delivering bottles and other tasks that probably never made any short list of tips on how to become a successful entrepreneur.

But I was learning the trade. Working hard. Studying a lot. And getting better at what I did.

I entered the small world of Parisian wine educators. Slowly but surely, companies started to hire me for their corporate functions. That is also when prestigious Hôtel de Crillon recruited me on their wine team. O Chateau was still a mess but a charming one since I managed to convince a friend and fellow rugby player to tag along in the adventure.

With Nicolas's arrival, one of the objectives was to turn this cute venture into a "real" company. "Real" was pursuing me. You know how rappers like to "keep it real". Well, realistically, I was below that. I was yet to make it real[6].

---

[6] To read more about whatever happened to O Chateau, please revert to the appendix (p.200)

CHAPTER 2

The road to pleasure and knowledge

Learning about wine

One small detail about deciding that my career would be in wine was to learn about it in the first place. Contrarily to what many people think, wine knowledge is not something you're born with in France. French DNA is relatively unsurprising to that extent.

To tackle the task of learning about wine, I decided to follow the recommendation a rugged sommelier had given me: *"If you want to learn about wine, just learn about wine"*. His abrupt take on wine education sounded good to me: I was tired of school and strongly believed that a few good books, hard work and mad resolution could go a long way.

So on I went. After a few months, I had the basics covered. My real problem appeared when I realized that studying wine was not just about Pinot Noir or Merlot, but also about plant biology, chemistry, history, geography, marketing, agronomy, etc. If I wanted to be good at what I did, I had a great deal to learn.

Getting serious about wine is quite the time-consuming endeavor[7]. Most people whom you may view as wine experts are usually just good at one thing: winemakers are good at making wine, sommeliers at talking about it, and wine journalists at drinking it for free. Heck, I'm a so-called expert now but trust me, if you had me run a winery, the wine I'd make would be more likely to make you blind than jolly.

Wine loving

Deciding to teach myself was a(nother) strange decision but one I am thankful for to this day. Simply because it helped me understand how dull learning about wine could be. How boring many wine books are, how mortifying most wine experts tend to be.

Maybe I ODed on wine geek gatherings but I'll happily confess that all these people going on and on about whether this wine smells like tobacco or blackcurrants just bores me to death. I like to taste, to feel, to travel with the smells and the textures, but I don't like to talk on and on about them. I want to experience and to live first hand!

When I visited star winemaker Michel Chapoutier in the Rhône Valley a few years ago, he shared a story with me. He told me how one day, he was tasting wine with one of his young interns. The intern, probably to show Michel how skilled he was, started delivering a very technical, systematic analysis of the wine they were tasting, breaking

---

[7] Don't you worry now, this book should offer a whole lot of helpful information collected over the years.

down every aspect of it. Michel stopped him in the middle of his speech: *"Boy, I'll tell you what: if you have sex like you taste wine, your girlfriend must be bored out of her mind!"*

And it is true: a wine lover should be quite literally a lover for wine. Wine drinking is eminently sensual: it doesn't invite us to intellectualize and to boast, but instead to let go and enjoy this delectable dispossession. Good wines should talk to our soul just as much as to our palate. To be true to them, what we need to do is shut the hell up!!

Now, if I had any form of coherence at all, that would be the end of this book. But for the sake of the hard-earned money you spent on it, I'll keep going, how's that?

Wine confidence

I find it amusing that most people feel confident in their ability to make educated comments about politics or religion – but not wine.

Most people know with high levels of certainty which politician is good for their country, but they would never be bold enough as to say which wine is good with sushi.

As soon as you start drinking wine, you keep getting bugged by the same issue of picking it. Any wine list, any wine shop, any wine aisle in a supermarket showcases the tremendous diversity and reminds us how little we know.

Enjoying wine seems to come with the pressing necessity to learn more about it. And surely enough, sooner or later, those who did will brag, and those who didn't will feel bad. When we drink wine, the lazy half of our Western brain tells us, *"Don't worry about it, you like this one, just enjoy it, that's really all you need to do*", while the other half whispers, "*You can't really just be ignorant about wine. Plus, you gotta keep up with Mike*[8]".

Because there is always a Mike. Even the most admirable of wine professionals have their own Mike. Even though most Mikes bore me, it turns out my job became being a Mike. Which implied to out-Mike all the other Mikies. Which meant learning also about the petty stuff: was 1989 a better year on the left bank or on the right bank of Bordeaux? Which Cabernet Franc clone is planted there? Which rootstock?[9], etc.

But this fantastic learning experience, this wonderful journey in the wine world has been a life-changing one for me. Wine has changed me – and it has changed my vision of the world. I guess that's what I'd like to share with you in this book: what I consider truly interesting in what I've gleaned along the way.

You be the judge.

France + California

Quickly after I started gaining a serious interest in wine, I spent a few months working in California. I found myself enthusiastic about the Californian approach to wine: keeping wine drinking fun, making wines more readable–I thought that was refreshing and truly exciting.

It seemed to me that France and its utter wine seriousness had a lesson or two to learn from California: many people in the French wine world took themselves too seriously, I thought; and if

---

[8] That annoying brother-in-law who's really into wine. People love him because "he always picks great wine" – jerk!
[9] And to be honest with you, I have very little interest in that kind of stuff – so you won't find much of it in this book.

they wanted to convince new people to drink their wine, they had better make the whole thing a bit more fun.

A few years later, as I learned more, as I continued my journey in wine, my relationship to the European wine culture evolved. I had known about its depth and its diversity for a while, and, as a native, I had intuitively cared for it. But it took me a few years to understand not only the beauty of the message this complexity carried but also to see the path it was unveiling.

As much as many wine people like to oppose the French and Californian approaches to wine, I strongly believe in the power of reconciling them: getting people more comfortable with wine, but without sacrificing what makes wine inspiring, or what makes it interesting.

In this transatlantic inspiration, I began shaping my motto that good wine education was not about simplifying things, but instead about giving people the key to understand and appreciate the diversity of wine[10].

---

[10] In this book, I will try to do just that.

> **Back roads vs. Highways**
>
> On the road to wine culture, many well-off people prefer to jump straight onto the highway. Assuming that expensive bottles are the best ones out there, those are the ones they tend to favor.
> I have never been well-off, so I was forced to take the back roads, to try the lesser-known wines, the ones with affordable price tags, coming from strange regions, and minuscule vineyards, made with forgotten grape varieties, etc. Experiencing the bumps and turns of the wine back roads has led me to discover the true diversity and the real beauty of the wine world.
> I think it's a much better, more economical and more fun way to develop a great wine culture.

Grapes and words

Just like literature, wine takes time to learn. Before having access to the emotion of a stunning poem or to the vigor of a captivating novel, we all had to go through a long initiation. First, we need to learn the alphabet, the sound of each letter. In wine, that would be learning about the grapes and their characteristics. Then, once we master our letters, we need to learn the arrangements of letters, the pronunciation, the grammar, the structure of sentences. Now we can read. In wine, that would be the stage when we start noticing differences between two reds. You no longer drink wine: you start drinking *this* wine.

> **Pleasure & Patience**
>
> Without patience and interest, one will only have access to immediate pleasures—which are good, but much lower in quality than the pleasures gained over time. Drinking a great wine without the experience of having tasted lesser ones will resonate empty. Great wine becomes only *"good wine... I guess!"* Having a fantastic wine in your glass is like having a beautiful girl in your arms: You'll have richer pleasure and emotion if you've been courting that girl for months than if you've just met her at a club, that same night, drunk.

At this point, very few 6-year-olds can differentiate the quality of a novel by Faulkner from the autobiography of Paris Hilton. Chances are, a 6-year-old would actually prefer to read the latter. This is the stage in which our teachers and our parents make us read more, make us acquire knowledge. After a while, we get to know what type of books we prefer. Some stories bore us; some we like. In wine, that would be the moment when you start liking Merlot better than Cabernet Sauvignon, Chardonnay better than Pinot Grigio[11].

So now we've read a few books. We're no longer the kids who didn't know their alphabet. Now we can look at things with a different angle. We're richer from experiences. Our judgment skills have

---

[11] Or the other way around!

been sharpened. Our tastes are more refined. We know the genres, the authors. We explore them.

With wine, that's the period when your culture has expanded again after a trip to Napa, to Tuscany, or after you've regularly frequented a good wine shop.

As with literature, the sheer beauty of wine will not be revealed to you immediately. It takes drinking quite a few bottles, over time, to get an "hmmm". It takes a few more to get a "wow". We need to be acquainted with mediocrity to notice greatness. Emotions in wine have a price: that of patience.

Booooo...

Well, that's a downer! No one wants to hear that you'll get good at something if you dedicate time, money and attention to it.

We live in this world of *"Buy this book or watch this video and you'll know everything you need to know"*. And we actually sort of believe it.

But what if, little emotion after little emotion, the impressionist wine painting each of us creates was more satisfying, more eye-opening, more exciting, than this 'very best' wine? What if the journey was more important than the destination? There is a true pleasure in experiencing something and realizing that your knowledge, your personal story, makes it even more enjoyable. The taste of things, their value, how they resonate: all this is not exterior to ourselves. We vastly carry them inside. This fantastic Oregon Pinot will only be more fantastic if you are an experienced Oregon Pinot drinker. The experience will genuinely be yours. You won't have inherited it. You will have woven it for yourself.

No matter who tells you the contrary, there is simply no shortcut to get to that form of satisfaction. But there is a road. And a long, and very enjoyable journey. One that taught me that drinking wine is not about making sense out of the mystery, but about chasing it instead.

> **Parisian intimacy**
>
> For one year when I was a student, the walk from the Métro to my school took me on a bridge over the Seine River. Twice a day, I would cross the Seine, in the morning, and at night. With the light, the rain, the wind, the reflections of the sun on the water, the Seine was always different. Every single time.
>
> After a few months, the Seine and I became intimate. I could notice differences. I could be touched. Tourists around thought that the Seine was beautiful. It was. But I had a deeper vision, enriched by experience, magnified by proximity. I had the privilege of knowing the Seine a bit more, of being touched by it in a different way, every day. I was awakened to emotion.
>
> With wine, it works the same way, the more wines you've tasted in your life, the deeper your emotion, and your relationship with it, will be. Back in those days, many students in my class would also take the same daily walk from the Métro to school. I'm sure a few others looked at the Seine every day.
>
> Those of us who did managed each day to get some more pleasure out of life, managed for a second to re-enchant our lives. We managed to make poetry exhale from the city.
>
> A pretty and costless form of selfishness.

PART 2

A journey from the soil to the soul

Getting to the bottom of the wine thing

> *"If you can't explain it to a six year old, you don't understand it yourself."*
> — Albert Einstein

I have no idea how a car works. So every time I go to a garage, with my proper city-boy looks, I'm just a sitting duck waiting to make all the wrong decisions[22].

A lot of people feel the same way with wine. So let me reassure you: I've done the homework and I can guarantee that getting better at wine[23] is much easier than most imagine. Truthfully, wine culture is not that impenetrable.

Wine is a story of transformations. In the coming chapters, we'll explore these transformations: we'll learn about the mysterious mechanisms by which a bit of soil, air, water and light are turned into the most enchanting of treats. One by one, we'll connect the wine dots to help you achieve a deeper understanding of wine and of its culture.

We'll take it from the very beginning, starting with the birth of the grapes, then we'll follow step by step the process that leads to the creation of a wine, from the grape growing, to the winemaking,

---

[22] At best.
[23] Whatever that means.

all the way to —my personal favorite— the wine ~~drinking~~ tasting!!

This fascinating journey will help us gain a better understanding of wine. It will also help us grasp the bigger picture of what there is to learn, not only about wine, but also, more importantly, from it.

INTO WINE

CHAPTER 3

Secrets of the Soil

> **The soil...**
> **First, let's learn *about* it.**

"It's a kind of magic."
— Queen

Down to earth

If you want to understand wine, the first thing to do is look down, for the story begins down there, in the soil.

The general idea is that in order to make wine, you need grapes, and in order for the vine to produce grapes, it needs food. Most of that food[24] comes from the soil.

Now, I was raised in Paris, so for all I knew, whatever was underneath the concrete, sidewalks

---

[24] Besides water, CO2 and sunlight.

and pavement was soil. Or dirt. Or Earth. Or whatever that brown stuff was called.

Studying wine taught me that there was a very big difference between soil and dirt: dirt is to soil what zombies are to humans. Soil is full of life, while dirt is devoid of it.

The soil teems with life: one gram of soil contains over 600 billion microorganisms that range from ugly little critters (worms, caterpillars, louse, spider, and mites), all the way to even uglier but microscopic elements (bacteria, fungi, enzymes, etc). Each one of them has a specific role; each one performs a specific duty in the incredible chain of actions that is going to provide the food that the vine needs.

Worms' awesomeness

Before becoming a major bumper-sticker figure, Charles Darwin was a keen student of worms[25]. He described them as the most important species in all of the animal reign (that is of course because hipsters did not exist in 1882), by their weight[26], and also by their activity.
You may legitimately wonder how it could possibly be so. Well, your typical worm day consists of eating dirt, traveling to the surface, and pooping. Then doing that again. And again. And again. This routine fulfills two crucial roles: keeping the soil alive[27], and fertilizing it[28].
If you compare the soil to a living organism, worms would be the intestines. Without them, the soil would die, which would result in no more wine.

---

[25] In 1882, he wrote a book called *The formation of vegetable mould through the action of worms, with observations on their habits.*

Gotta love a creeper!

It took me a while to understand why when I said, "a vine is a creeper", young American girls would giggle. So no, a vine does not stare at you while you sleep. It's actually quite rare for vines to show any form of interest in young American girls at all. Their thing, truly, is eating and drinking[29].

And to satisfy these needs, vines don't use daddy's credit card, but instead—call them traditional—they work for it. Specifically, that means they develop a root system. These roots[30] are going to explore the soil[31], seeking the water[32] and nutrients the vine needs.

> **Did You Know:**
> A buckwheat plant can produce up to 125 miles of roots.
>
> A rye-wheat plant can produce up to 350 miles of roots (that is over 1 billion miles of roots per acre).
>
> The roots of an oak tree can dig 400 feet deep.

---

[26] Which equates to that of all other species put together.
[27] By allowing oxygen to flow through the tunnels worms dig.
[28] His daily routine of defecating tunnel digger and dirt eater brings back organic matter (rich in calcium, potassium, magnesium) to the surface, which helps make the soil more fertile.
[29] Sounds familiar?
[30] Sometimes up to 150 feet below the ground (that is quite deep)
[31] And subsoil
[32] I know – disappointing, right!

The taste of soil

When I first started to be a wine educator, I lacked the delicate know-how of how to deal with wine snobs. An old timer gave me the best tip: "*Cut them off right away. Don't let them go on. Tell them they're wrong, even if they're not. Otherwise, they'll never shut up*". I have ever since adopted the, "*Well, sir, what you say is interesting but it's actually not fully accurate*".

One thing a lot of wine snobs[33] like to say is that the wine tastes like the soil it comes from: a soil of clay will give that chalky something to the wine, a soil of granite that flinty taste, etc.

Well, what they say is interesting but it's actually not fully accurate! (Smooth, huh?) Simply because between the soil and the vine, there is a middleman: bacteria.

Now rest assured: if you think you were bad at chemistry, well, I was the guy who was even worse than you. So let me break it down for you.

Soil 〉 Bacteria 〉 Vine 〉 Grapes 〉 Wine

Imagine a mother with her baby. The baby is not old enough to ingest meat[35], so Nature asks the mother to do her part: *she* needs to be eating the meat so that her body can synthesize it and pass on the nutrients to the baby, though her milk.

---

[33] And wine professionals alike.
[35] Even if you turn meat into meat powder, the baby is not equipped physiologically to synthesize the proteins of meat.

Same exact story for wine. Except that between the soil and the grape, you'll find bacteria. Without bacteria[36], the vine would not be able to absorb the food the soil has to offer.[37]

> **Implications for wine**
>
> Great wines bring something else to the table, something frequently referred to as complexity. The complexity of a wine is merely a mirror of the complexity of the microbiological life of its soil.
>
> What we perceive as the taste of wine is organic compounds. To come to life, these organic compounds need all the resources the soil has to offer. If the soil is unhealthy, the potential of the wine will necessarily be limited.
>
> In short, no great wines from unhealthy soil.

---

[36] Also worth mentioning is another tool vines use to process food from the soil. Particular soil fungi called mycorrhizae will help the roots absorb phosphorus, zinc or calcium, in exchange from some carbohydrates provided by the vine. Underground business!

[37] So when you think about it, bacteria could be viewed as the mother of the vine. Mamma Bacteria!!

> **The soil...**
> **Alright, now, let's learn *from* it.**

Talk dirt(y) to me

The outcome of this microscopic subterranean ballet is nothing less than the creation of life on the surface of our planet. Without the soil, there would be —let alone no wine— no water to drink[38], no food to eat[39] and no air to breathe[40].

Soil truly is a fabulous place, and a very frugal one too: it simply captures a bit of light, water and CO2 and in return offers all the plants, all the trees, all the flowers, all the fruits, all the proteins, all the sugars, all the tastes, all the smells... and all the wines at the surface of our planet.

Simply put, life pulsates from the soil.

Pesti... what?

I must say that until I learned more about how the soil worked, killing "pests" sounded pretty good to me.

---

[38] Soil is what makes water potable. By passing over and through the soil, water becomes purified.
[39] We humans eat plants and animals. Without soil, there are no plants (and therefore no animals, since they too need plants).
[40] Through photosynthesis, plants liberate the oxygen we breathe.

Pest: insect, or weed, parasite
Cide: from Latin *caedere,* "murder, kill"

However, the soil being such an eminently complex environment, I learned that there is no such a thing as the good guys, and the bad guys down there. Killing such or such inhabitants of the soil comes with both short and long-term consequences.

> **Deliberate simplifications**
>
> Nature has very efficient defense mechanisms that render the use of pesticides vastly counter-productive in the long run.
> Using pesticides will eliminate a great deal of the targeted population (insects, small animals, bacteria, etc.). However, a small percentage of resistant individuals shall survive. Their genetic programming makes it so that when their environment becomes threatening, they will procreate more in order to ensure survival of their species.
> An indirect consequence of using pesticides is the fast increase in the population that is resistant to that type of pesticide.

But business is business[41]: more than 45 billion dollars are now spent each year on soil-destroying pesticides.[42]

---

[41] Well, technically, it's more like "poorly regulated business is business"...
[42] In the world. Source: BCC Research (and yup, that is a B).

INTO WINE

CHAPTER 4

Gentleman Farming

> **Farming...
> First, let's learn *about* it.**

"I am fond of pigs. Dogs look up to us. Cats look down on us. Pigs treat us as equals."
— Winston S. Churchill

It's not that fancy!

The soil gives us vines: we're one step closer to having wine. But vine is a fragile little thing, one that requires work and attention. This is why farming is an absolutely essential part of the creation of a wine.

INTO WINE

Most outsiders view the world of wine as the reign of elegance, refinement and culture. Truth is: making wine starts with painstaking and humbling tasks performed all year on the vineyard. There is no good wine without good grapes, and there are no good grapes without good farming.

Grape growers are farmers. The French word *vignerons*[44] says just that: the *vigneron* is the person in charge of working the vine. Many people in the wine world therefore define themselves as farmers, which, let's face it, doesn't sound quite right when you hear it from the owner of some fancy Château in Bordeaux, while he's driving you around his property at the wheel of his Bentley (as Golda Meir once said: "Don't be so modest, you're not that great!"). On the other side of the spectrum, some more salt-of-the-earth *vignerons* push the farming logic to the limit: when Mark Angeli[45], who happens to be one of the greatest wine talents in France emailed me his price list[46], I discovered that it featured not only the price for his whites or his rosés, but also for his flour, his apple juice and his chickens. When I called to order some wine from him, his voicemail just said, "Try me again after dusk!"[47].

Since farming is the very foundation of making wine, it is very enlightening to learn more about how the grapes are farmed; it is in fact certainly

---

[44] The French word for winegrower, someone who cultivates grapes. I'll use it throughout the book also because it corresponds to a rural and sociological reality of small independent growers that don't just grow and sell their grapes but instead make their own wine as well. Basically, creating their wine from the vineyard to the bottle.
[45] From the *Ferme de la Sansonnière* in the Loire Valley.
[46] Actually, his son Martial did. Seems like Mark dabbles with grapes better than with computers.
[47] Music to this city boy's ear.

the most potent way to decode a lot of the BS infused in the wine world.

> **Farming year round**
>
> Fall: pruning of the vine starts; in colder regions, you may also "hill-up" the soil around the feet of the vines to protect them from the upcoming cold.
> Winter: pruning continues. It is a long and painstaking activity (lasts several months) but a crucial one for the quality of the future wine.
> Spring: Spreading of fertilizers and pesticides; tying, which involves attaching the vines to the wire[48] for plant stability and for maximum sun/air exposure.
> Summer: Removing unwanted shoots; more tying; crop thinning as needed; spraying of sulfur and other sprays; green harvest.[49]
> Late Summer/Fall: Harvest.

The Old School

When it comes to farming, there are of course many ways to operate.

In the traditional way of farming [50] that prevailed for millennia worldwide, farmers would farm crops and raise animals that would work well given their particular environment. Grape growing was usually just one of many activities.

---

[48] Called trellis.
[49] Only for vineyards interested in quality over quantity. Green harvests mean you're going to cut the first grapes coming out in order to have the vine focus its energy on a lower number of grapes.
[50] Be it a vineyard, a field of cereals or of vegetables.

To protect their crop, or to make their land more fertile, techniques depended on what was efficient and available locally[51].

It was old school, but it worked[52].

The New School

> *"A nation that destroys its soils destroys itself.*
> — Franklin D. Roosevelt

Everything changed with the great boom of chemistry in the 19th and 20th centuries. Fertilizers and pesticides of all sorts (insecticides, fungicides, herbicides—you name it) ceased to be derived from natural and local resources but started instead being engineered by big chemicals corporations and sold to farmers.

Results at first seemed wonderful. Imagine a young teenage boy discovering steroids and suddenly getting really popular with girls. What's not to like, right?

Unfortunately, there is always a flipside. In the case of steroids, they make your 'man parts' shrink; in that of man-made fertilizers and pesticides, they slowly but surely kill your soil[53].

---

[51] For example, to fertilize their land, some would spread bones or ashes, others would opt for human or animal manure. To protect their land, subterfuges like sulfur, arsenic, or tobacco have been used for centuries.

[52] Though it didn't spare farmers ans populations from occasional years of hunger and devastation

[53] Not to mention that intensive agriculture is a model based entirely on oil. Oil to heat up greenhouses, to run tractors, to manufacture fertilizers, pesticides, packaging, etc. As an example, it takes approximately three tons of petrol to create one ton of nitrogen-based fertilizer.

It is—one must admit—a brilliant business model[54]. It looks somewhat like this:

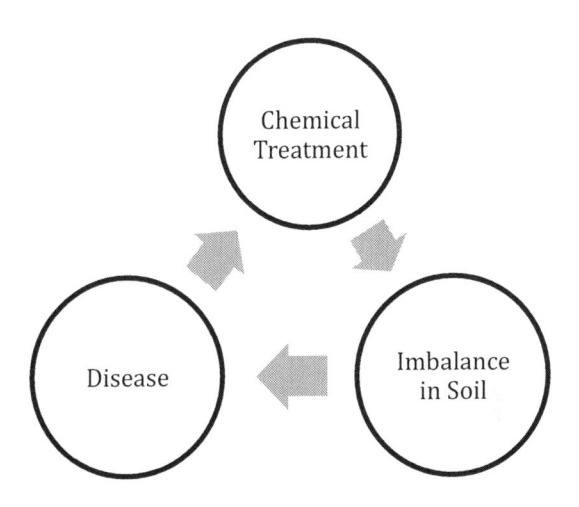

```
        Chemical
        Treatment
       ↗         ↘
   Disease  ←  Imbalance
                in Soil
```

When you know that healthy soil is not only what makes wine good, but also marginally what makes life on Earth possible, this gets interesting.

How about the wine world?

In the farming world, the wine world is a bit like that innocent looking boy who actually behaves just as badly as his friends, but looks so cute and proper.

At the wake of the seventies, our innocent looking wine world also took the chemical turn and started treating vines with man-made fertilizers and pesticides.

You can be sure that when this one guy who takes steroids starts getting noticed by most girls

---

[54] From any other point of view, it's quite despicable really.

in school, by the end of the school year, a vast majority of students will have bigger biceps than the PE teacher. That is exactly what happened – except that instead of steroids, the drug for grape growers was chemical fertilizers and pesticides and instead of more girls, the incentive was less work for them and less people on the payroll.

Surely, there were a few people who were wary of these guys in suits coming to their vineyards to sell them some miraculous chemicals. But the most reluctant usually ended up falling for it after seeing how flattering their neighbors' newly weeded vineyard looked[55].

Big Business 1 – Terroir 0.

So where do we stand now?

"There is more bacteriological activity in the soils of the Sahara than in some French vineyards."
Claude Bourguignon[56]

The world of wine as a whole has become a dunce.[57] A vast majority of grapes used to make wine have been and are still loaded with pesticides.

---

[55] The simple explanation to this is that herbicides kill the soil's microorganisms. Consequently, when they die, they make up a sort of natural yet very temporary fertilizer. So right after it was sprayed with pesticides for the first time, the vineyard was artificially doped, and indeed looked better for a few weeks – usually enough time to convince everyone around to buy these chemicals.

[56] Soil Scientist (can't recommend enough looking into he and his wife's Lydia's work). Cited by Nicolas Joly in *Wine from sky to Earth*.

[57] In Europe only cereal growers do worse than viticulturists (Source: FAOSTAT). In 2006, grapes accounted for 3.5% of the farmed land in the European Union and used up 15% of the pesticides. These numbers ought to be qualified, as

> **Toxic Vino**
>
> If a vineyard is sprayed with pesticides, are these substances ultimately found in the wine?
> For a number of them, the answer[58] is yes. You will hear people telling you that there is no need to worry because the maximum authorized limits are not reached. And this is very true.
> Especially since there is no such thing as a maximal authorized limit for wine (and those for grapes are very high). Interestingly though, a study on the presence of pesticide residues in wine[59] indicated that some samples[60] showed levels of pesticides that were 5,800 times higher than the maximum authorized concentration for tap water.
> I'll pass!

I remember on a recent trip to the Californian wine country that we were asked by the lady escorting our party to please stay away from the vineyard because a man wearing a yellow biohazard suit and mask was "treating" it. So not OK to get near the chemicals, but clearly OK to drink them. On your typical vineyard[60], such treatments occur ten to twenty times a year.

So much for the life of the soil, so much for *terroir*!

---

viticulturists use metals like copper or sulfur, which require significant doses. Toxicity of chemicals used should certainly come into the equation of such calculations.

[58] Presented in 2008 by Pesticide Action Network Europe.

[59] Samples came from all across the world, all available for sale in Europe. The study doesn't indicate which wine(s) scored the worst.

[60] This applies to non-organic vineyards – I'll come back to it.

A hidden gem

Some of my favorite French wines are produced by the Château de Chavanes in the Jura region.
They planted their vines on parcels of land that had been abandoned for a long time. Consequently, their soil had not been exposed to decades of chemicals.
On a soil full of life, they make absolutely stunning wines.

> **Farming...**
> **Alright, now, let's learn *from* it.**

"Only after the last tree has been cut down, only after the last river has been poisoned, only after the last fish has been caught, only then will you discover that money cannot be eaten."
— Native American Saying

"The planet is fine. The people are fucked."
— George Carlin

Bigger than wine

When you like wine, and start to learn more about it, you quickly realize that the soil makes a difference. Studying how vineyards were farmed has helped me grasp that the importance of the soil actually goes far beyond wine, and that the implications of mistreating it are also much more far-reaching that we think.

Under the combined effects of chemical pesticides, chemical fertilizers, deep plowing and tractors, we've managed to eradicate most of the life of our soils. Even though it may come across as unchanged on the surface, the truth is that for the most part, our soil has now turned to dirt.

After a few decades of mining our soils instead of farming them, we have destroyed them[61].

Messing with the soil is a gigantic mistake—and Nature has already started to get back at us for it.

Six unsuspected effects of pesticides

1) Floods:

Have you ever wondered why even though we live in such a dry era, we have so many floods? It doesn't seem to make sense. Well, to understand this, you must know that when it rains, most of the water is absorbed by the soil[62], while the rest streams away. But what happens in places where the soil is dead is that the soil is not able to fulfill its absorption function properly. Consequently, most of the rainwater ends up streaming away. Mechanically, in case of heavy rain, rivers overflow and towns get flooded.

Interestingly enough, we relentlessly blame the rain!!

2) Desertification:

After intoxicating our soils, they end up infertile. In the world today, we destroy 25 million acres of farmland every year (plus another 12 million that we build upon).[63] Every single minute that goes by,

---

[61] In places where the farmer can still afford fertilizers, plants still come out of it, in others, the land is simply abandoned.
[62] That's (also) what the soil does.
[63] Each year, according to IFEN (*Institut Français de l'Environnement*), France loses 150,000 acres of soil every year, with 90% of these to the detriment of farmland. In 2011, France destroyed over 400 acres of land a day.

47 acres of soil are abandoned. That is 463 times the size of Manhattan each year[64].

3) Destruction of rural life:

In Western countries, farmers took the bait of mechanization and chemicals; this led them to substantial debt levels[65], while food prices kept going down[66]. In a matter of years, most were financially asphyxiated and went out of business. In poorer nations, a similar system was introduced. Small farmers can no longer feed their family or their community. They are forced to give up their ancestral lifestyle only to grow the populations of one of the many slums of the world. Other option for them is death: in India over the past decade, 200,000 farmers committed suicide. That is one every 30 minutes, every single day, for ten years. It is a silent genocide.

(I know, this is a really jolly part of the book – but stick with me: solutions are coming. We can't just simply turn a blind eye to all this).

4) Famine:

In the world today, over one billion people are suffering from hunger.[67] Yup, B again.

---

[64] This being amplified by irrigation. In drier regions, farmers no longer stick to growing plants and raising animals that are adapted to their *terroir*, and as such, economical with water. For them, irrigation has become a necessity: rainwater is no longer enough. Problem is, the water used to irrigate is generally taken from groundwater. But as opposed to rainwater, groundwater contains salts. By irrigating, farmers salinize their soil and thus slowly kill it.
[65] Tractors don't come in cheap
[66] Due to overproduction
[67] "In 2009, the number of people suffering from hunger in the world went up 105 million compared to 2008, and the

5) Pollution of rivers and groundwater:

With the worm population dying massively, their activity is now left vastly undone. So the elements that worms usually bring back up to the surface like nitrogen or phosphates are no longer brought up to the surface. Consequently, we end up finding them in our groundwater and rivers.

6) Hurricanes:

In order to compensate for the millions of acres of farmland we lose each year, we deforest millions of acres in places like Brazil, Cambodia or Nigeria. One immediate consequence there is a dramatic increase in temperature.

Anyone who has ever taken a stroll in the woods on a sunny afternoon knows how much cooler temperature in the woods is compared to temperature out in the open. Well, multiply this by several million acres and you end up with a sudden and significant hike in temperatures around the equator. In the meantime, temperatures around the poles don't go up as fast. Can you hear the wind blowing already?

If you combine all these elements, very few of us can say that they have not been affected, directly or through a friend or a family member, by these issues.

Realizing that the way the treat our soil is responsible for all these tragedies, I now think twice before calling them "natural" phenomena.

---

numbers are over one billion now." - Jacques Diouf, - Director of the FAO (UN's food and agriculture organization) - April 2010.

Simple solutions to fix our soil

Good news is, solutions to regenerate our soil do exist. On the farm, or the vineyard, the following practices are wonderful starting points:

Composting:
By returning organic matter to the land, farmers can slowly but surely regenerate the life of their soil.

Ramial Chipped Wood:
By spreading a layer of chipped wood on their soil, they offer it a real feast, which leads to a dramatic increase in soil health and fertility.

Balancing cultures:
By moving away from strict monocultures, farmers will offer habitats and resources for the fauna and flora necessary to create a healthy environment.

These solutions sure necessitate extra work and sometimes extra money[68], but what they really require is a shift in the way farmers view their profession and their business.

Inevitably, cultivating the land thus becomes much more intellectually challenging, environmentally sustainable, financially viable[69] (sorry, needed an adverb fix) and therefore attractive in every way.

---

[68] Especially in the case of Ramial Chipped Wood, which, without subsidies, is only applicable to crops yielding significant potential profits, like grapes.

[69] Should you want to support this cause, you may write to your state representative and ask them what they're doing to ban pesticides.

Simply put, moving away from the way we currently farm the land is not only utterly necessary and urgent, it is also very much possible[70].

---

[70] A little help from governments would be awesome, but let's be realistic here!

CHAPTER 5

Terroir: the keystone to wine

> **Terroir...
> First, let's learn *about* it.**

Geography professors

Mark Twain once wrote "God created war so that Americans would learn geography." The French were already set: they had wine. For centuries, wine has been their geography professor. And it's been a great one, for really, there is no greater incentive to learn about geography than the promise that your knowledge is going to be turned into a great wine.

Spending months and years farming a vineyard is a bit like spending a lot of time with a friend. After a while, you start knowing her better. You know that this smirk means frustration, that this shoulder shrug comes with jolliness or that this song on the radio means crank it up! Well, same goes for a vineyard: attentive farming gives you access to the same intimacy. You notice the change in the leaves' color mid-hill, you realize that the soil is more damp on this parcel, you notice that birds like to fly around that section of the vineyard, etc. In short, you realize that you vineyard is not uniform.

So century after century, European vineyards were observed and patiently mapped out: some parcels were identified as making beautiful grapes and therefore great wine, others as being more relevant for mediocre wine. These subdivisions became known as... *terroirs*.

Damn French words

I will stay true to my zero jargon commitment but I'll request one free pass from you: and that is for the word *terroir*.

Simply because there is no understanding wine[71] if you don't have a good grasp of what *terroir* means. In short, it goes like this:

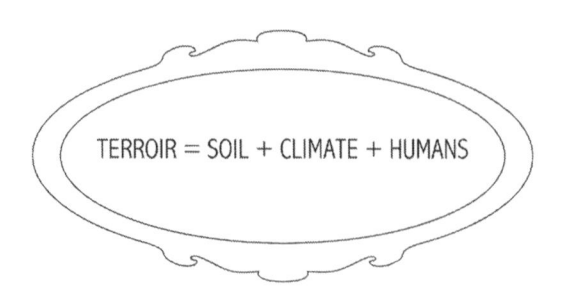

TERROIR = SOIL + CLIMATE + HUMANS

Terroir is the essence of a place – its signature. It is what's unique, non-reproducible, and singular

---

[71] Or anything wine-related.

about a particular vineyard. *Terroir* is what makes one place different from another one. It encompasses three main elements:

1) **Soils:** What's on top and what's further below[72]
2) **Climates:** microclimate and macroclimate[73]
3) **Humans:** the locals and their know-how[74]

Each element has a direct influence on the grapes, and as such, potentially, on the resulting wine.

If I used *terroir* in a non-wine way, I would say for instance that the *terroir* of the American South at the beginning of the last century gave us jazz just like that of Brooklyn in the 1980s gave us hip-hop.

Cool? Cool!

No *terroir* without humans

> *"The role of the terrain in the making of a Grand Cru doesn't go much beyond that of matter in the making of a work of art."*
> – Roger Dion[75]

As much as the *Terroir = Soil + Climate* equation seems to make sense, the human part, let's face it, appears a bit shady.

---

[72] Called respectively pedology and geology
[73] Climate of that particular place and year (windy on top of the hill, rainy Spring this year, etc) and general climate of the region (e.g. continental, oceanic, etc.)
[74] Which means not only the talent, inspirations and choices of people involved, but also the knowledge they inherited from the generations before them.
[75] In *Histoire de la Vigne* et du vin des origines au XIXe siècle.

Yet, it is indeed a critical one. Here's why: take one the most expensive wines in the world, Château Pétrus[76]. If it wasn't for the people that decided centuries ago to plant vines there, and then for the generations of others after them that worked that vineyard to produce beautiful wines, maybe what is today Château Pétrus would have become, who knows, a mall or a strip club.

Terroir is about the place, and as such, it's also about the people. (Which by the way also includes us, the wine drinkers, because realistically, if it wasn't for a few nut bags like us willing to spend 20, 30, 40, 50 or more on a bottle of what is really just fermented grape juice, there would be none of this fancy *terroir* thing going on.)

The *savoir-faire* (know-how) of the *vigneron* needs the *savoir-boire* (know-how... to drink) of the wine drinker. Team work: they make it, we drink it! My kind of sport!!

---

[76] One bottle usually sells for 4 digits.

> **The case of irrigation**
>
> One of the biggest enemies of the expressions of terroir in wine is irrigation. When you feed water to the vine[70], roots grow infantilized: they no longer need to dig deep to go find water in the depths of the soil.
> Consequently, the root system grows horizontally instead of vertically. Meaning most roots remain close to the surface, in the superficial layer of the soil, and don't go explore. This does not mean the wine won't be good, but simply that the expression of its terroir will be limited to non-existent.[80]

Terroirs everywhere

> *"Terroir is a terrain, with a guy on it"*[80]
> – Denis Dubourdieu[81]

There is no translation for *terroir* in English—or in any other language for that matter. I love these words that just can't be translated from language to language. They seem dignified, grounded, battling against the imperialism of reality.

---

[78] Generally through a system called drip-irrigation.
[79] Interestingly enough, while it is a very common practice in most of the wine world, for AOC wine in France, irrigation is illegal (more on what AOC's are in chapter 8). This is one of the causes for the more frequent expression of *terroir* in many French wines.
[80] That was my poor translation of *"Un terroir*, c'est un terrain avec un bonhomme dessus ».
[81] Winemaker, Researcher and Professor of Oenology at the University of Bordeaux.

Yet, *terroirs* exist all over the world.[82] France has some great *terroirs*, and so does California, Australia, Italy, New Zealand, or any other country. Reversely, France also has some pretty crappy *terroirs* and so do all other countries out there.

When it comes to *terroir*, the main advantage France beholds (besides the fact that we're pretty good at pronouncing the word correctly) is history. The legendary *terroirs* of France [83] have been discovered, shaped and worked upon century after century.

In "New World"[84] countries, where vine and wine culture is more recent, the work of identification and expression of great *terroirs* is only starting. Some have already been identified, some not[85]. In China for instance, ardent work is currently being performed by billionaires and big wine corporations alike to identify the country's most promising *terroirs*.

---

[82] Proof: wine lovers and professionals worldwide have adopted the word as such, without translating it.
[83] Montrachet, Pomerol, Clos de Vougeot, Pauillac, etc.
[84] Expression that came up in the seventies to designate: Australia, USA, South Africa, Argentina, Chile, and New-Zealand.
[85] And others are not interpreted to the best of their potential yet.

Terroirs, Money and History

As much as we like to romanticize nature, a quick look at history teaches us that many wine regions have first and foremost an urban essence. Before anything else, Chianti was and still is the vineyard of Florentines: if it wasn't back in the days for the wealth of the banking and merchants families of Florence, for the infrastructures that facilitated the commerce of their wines, the entire world would have never known or fallen in love with Tuscan wines. Same story in Bordeaux, or more recently in Napa Valley, and who knows, tomorrow, in Brazil or India.

Terroir...
Alright, now, let's learn *from* it.

Throughout history, *terroirs* have given birth to countless fantastic wines. But the scope of *terroir* reaches far beyond wine: *terroir* is about the local environment. As such, it really is about local culture. There is no local culture without *terroir*, and no *terroir* without local culture.

The Terroir Machine

Fermentation is a complex process but also a fantastic 'terroir-expressing machine'. Products that are the result of a fermentation process have great potential to express the specificities of their terroir:

Fermented drinks:
wine (grapes)
cider (apples)
beer (cereals)
spirits (fruits, vegetables or cereals)

Products and drinks made from:
- fermented leaves or beans: coffee, chocolate, tea, tobacco
- fermented milk: cheeses
- cured meats and fish: charcuterie , smoked meats and fish

Putting *terroir* first

If we rewind to one century ago, each region and each country was rich with a particular type of drink [86] as well as a language of its own, a particular architecture, a unique gastronomy, special accents and artistic expressions, specific traditions and mythologies that were singular to that particular area of the world.

Today, our world has opened up significantly, and many of its local particularities have vanished: whether you're in New York, Rio, Paris, Moscow or Sydney, everywhere the same towers, the same hotel chains, restaurant chains, coffee shop chains, clothing chains, everywhere you find the same movies, the same TV shows, the same food, the same music.

Thus leaving us in a world that has grown to become more and more *terroir-less*.

Globalization vs. Globalism

Globalization: process of exchanges of material and immaterial goods and services made possible by innovation.

Globalism: ideological project aimed at dissolving all nations into a single unified humanity in order to durably establish a one-world government.

Unlike globalization, globalism carries the very ferments of uniformity for everything and everyone.

---

[86] Wine, beer, tea, you name it, all made locally according to the local *terroir*.

Preserving the community

Paris is my *terroir*[87], my beautiful urban *terroir*[88]. Over the past decades—in Paris like in many other places of the world—the local *terroir* has impoverished dramatically.

I've witnessed first hand with O Chateau how the best Parisian neighborhoods have become too expensive for small Parisian business owners or artisans[89]. One by one, independent book shops, bakeries, and cafés–essentially, the very *terroir* of Paris–closed down only to be replaced by the only ones that could afford to take over their lease—chain stores like McDonald's, H&M, Starbuck's, etc., triumphing once again.

At the same time we were destroying our soil, we were destroying our local cultures. Effects are equally staggering: as much as I hate to admit it, anyone claiming that France is the country of a proud, elegant and joyful people having copious amounts of great food and wine just need to get their facts straight[90].

Fortunately, wine taught me that there was another way.

---

[87] My first book '*Stuff Parisians Like*' recounts, in a cheeky fashion, the *terroir* of Paris today.
[88] Before crazy urban takeover, the Paris area used to be sprinkled with vineyards (Montmartre, Bercy, Suresnes, etc).
[89] Say you own a shop and you decide to retire. Even if you rent your space, you may take money from your successor to ensure that he will get your shop. Nowadays, it is not uncommon to have to pay well over one million euros upfront to rent a shop in a good central location in Paris.
[90] See box in the coming page. Such a dreadfully realistic appraisal bothers us. Rightly so. Spontaneous reaction is denial: "It can't be, you're exaggerating, there are so many cute little restaurants where food is great..." Naturally. But what's interesting is the bigger picture here.

Let's compare four pillars of French culture with actual figures and data—with a special focus on French youth:

Gastronomy: right after the US, McDonald's corporation's second most profitable country on Earth is France[92]. French youngsters eat sandwiches, pizzas, hamburgers and kebabs, thus they collapse slowly towards poisoning, obesity and ignorance of their own culinary patrimony.

Wine: France is the only country in the world where wine consumption has constantly decreased for the past 20 years. People will tell you that the French drink less but better. Actual figures shed a different light: in France, the average amount of money sent on a bottle of wine is inferior to 4€[93] (i.e. $5). Yearly wine budget (still+sparkling) for a French household is less than 200€ (i.e. $250)[94].
Of all age categories, youngsters are the ones who drink the least wine. Only 37% of young adults in France claim to like wine, but 92% happily share that they'd have beer or sodas over wine[95].

Fashion: the French have adopted the typical Westerner's uniform. It would be a lie to say that French people dress better or differently than other Westerners. As per French haute-couture, they're all close to one century old, their creative directors are generally foreigners and they make money thanks to their foreign clients.

Joie de vivre: in 2010, the French consumed over 130 million tablets of sleeping pills and antidepressants[96]. It is the most morose people on Earth[97]: the French are more pessimistic than the people of Afghanistan and Iraq. Only 5% of youngsters in France consider the future to be promising[98].

---

[91] See McDonald's Corp. Annual report

Cultural resistance

> "Knowing is not enough; we must apply.
> Willing is not enough; we must do."
> — Johann Wolfgang von Goethe

Harvest lunches tend to be epic moments, with dozens of pickers eating and drinking together. In artisanal French wineries, the husband is generally out in the vineyard making sure pickers are doing a good job, while the wife is inside cooking for the crew.

One year in Burgundy, tripe was on the menu: "They like it when I make tripe each year," Micheline shared with me. Seeing grapes pickers voraciously eating what most of this world's population would find beyond off-putting, I remember thinking to myself, "screw Parisian art exhibits: this is real culture!"

Local cultures keep communities alive. They also make for a much more diverse, much more interesting and much more fun world. If we want to keep that world alive, we need to be a part of it, and we need to support it.

---

[92] This figure did go up but only marginally. The increase is mostly due to the general increase of the price of wine due to galloping inflation and broader market.
[93] Source:*"Les achats de vin par les ménages français"* by Vinhiflor (2005).
[94] Cited by Emmanuel Delmas on Sommelier-vins.com – Thesis entitled *"Le Vin et les Jeunes"* by Julien Zilbermann
[95] Source rapport AFSSAPS – *Etats des lieux de la consommation de psychotropes en France* – 2012
[96] Gallup International Survey of expectations for 2012, cited in the Financial Times, "A Nation of pessimists" (May 5, 2012).
[97] Study entirled *La jeunesse face à l'avenir* by *Fondation pour l'Innovation Politique*.

In a world of fast foods, junk food and boring sandwiches, I believe that eating tripe is full of panache. It is an act of cultural resistance.

And you know what: I don't even like tripe!

> **The Power of Consumption Choices**
>
> - In 2000, Starbucks was opening one shop a day in the world.
> - After launching in Japan (1996) and China (1998), the company went for Australia (2000).
> - Starbucks was confident in its reputation and in its business-model and decided to start operating in Australia with no advertising, and by simply replicating its US offer.
> - In 2008, Starbucks had opened 84 shops throughout Australia.
> - Australia is a country with excellent coffee culture, so Australians soon enough started to turn their back to Starbucks. Profitability went down. Most Aussies deemed Starbucks coffee too expensive and too sugary. Many also resented the arrogant imperialistic approach that denied the specificities of the local market and culture.
> - Mid 2008, Starbucks HQ announced that they would shut down 61 out of the 84 Starbucks in Australia.

Challenging Goliaths is possible[98]. If we decide to preserve our own *terroirs*—be they on a vineyard or in big cities—victory (and joy) is around the corner.

---

[98] And very much necessary.

INTO WINE

CHAPTER 6

Super grapes!

> **The grapes...**
> **First, let's learn *about* them.**

*"Quality means doing it right
when no one is looking."*
— Henry Ford

Grapes galore

After a year of farming our various *terroirs*, vines usually[99] end us giving us grapes. We're one step closer to having wine!

There are in the world close to 9,600 different types of grapes. Out of all these, approximately 1,500 are relevant to make wine. Some grape

---

[99] Not always as hail for instance may wipe out an entire harvest in minutes.

varieties[100] are quite well known (Merlot, Pinot Noir, Chardonnay, etc.), others are completely under the radar[101].

Each type of grape comes with its own set of general characteristics. Some are lighter, some stronger, some are more velvety, some less, some have strong citrusy aromas, others give away notes of currants, etc. Think of apples: a granny smith is green and has this strong acidity and distinct "green apple" taste, a pink lady is yellow and red and has a softer edge to it: same story.

That is of course for the general identity. The *terroir* has a tremendous influence on the grapes and therefore on the wine made out of them: is your Chardonnay planted in a cool or warm climate region? On a hill or on the plain? On a soil of gravel or of granite?

Another key element we explored that explains the singularity of each wine is the way the vineyard has been farmed: has that soil been bombarded with chemical pesticides and fertilizers or is it alive and healthy?

In the end, the grape variety is just the raw material for your wine. Imagine someone asking you about this new house you just bought. You'd probably tell that person how many bedrooms your new house has, which neighborhood it's in, but you probably would not say, "It's wood and cement". For wine just like for houses, the raw material can only go so far. This is one of the reasons why on wine labels in Europe, we usually mention the region of origin, not the type of grapes[102].

---

[100] Also called varietals or *cépages* in French.
[101] Names like: Bastardo (Portugal), Dunkelfelder (Germany), Counoise (France), Öküzgözü (Turkey), Usakhelauri (Georgia), just to name a few.
[102] Bordeaux, Chianti, Champagne, Rioja, Tokay, etc. are not grape varieties, they are regions.

My organic 180

Like most people who were not raised by hippies, I did not grow up thinking that organic (which means farmed with no pesticides) was awesome. Finding myself to be a healthy young man, while eating lots of unhealthy food, I thought —quite brilliantly so— that organic was just another marketing scam designed for hipsters, rich people or gullible fools.

Studying wine, I grew to understand that I was completely wrong. I came to realize how crucial the life of the soil was and how organic agriculture, though not perfect[103], was a very positive step towards healthier soils, healthier food and a more sustainable future.

A lot of folks still have strong reservations[104] against "organic"[105], and specifically "organic wine".

---

[103] As with any form of official labeling, some take advantage of it and sneak around the looseness of its definition or lobby in its favor: organic labels at a French, European or American level don't mean the same thing. It is also possible to grow "organically" on unhealthy soil.

[104] In case you wonder why organic suffers such bad reputation, simply look at who the main clients of most media outlets are: in 2011, according to Kantar Media, the total amount of advertising money spent in the USA alone by Food, Candy and Restaurant companies exceeded 12 billion dollars. That's over 30 million dollars spent on advertising each day. Not a whole lot of "watch out for food loaded with pesticides" on TV! And since I'm not cheeky, I won't even mention the advertising budget spent by pharmaceutical firms...

[105] Side note: the goal of this book is not to get into a comprehensive description of the world of "organic " farming and labels. Many of these labels are indeed surprisingly loose but getting into that would be a whole different book.

I hope the previous chapters convinced you that what's at stake in the choice of what we eat and drink, and how we farm goes far beyond these petty considerations.

Grapes, whether they are farmed with or without pesticides, do not necessarily lead to a good wine because it takes a lot of work, skills and luck, both in the vineyard and at the winery for wine to be good. So there are some bad organic wines, and there are also plenty of delicious ones. All in all, what's for sure is that they are usually better for you than non-organic ones[106].

---

[106] It should be noted that a majority of organic grape growers use copper, whitewash or artificial pheromones. Organic growing does allow all this. Thus showing that organic should not be viewed as a new practice or religion aiming for purity or perfection, but instead as a path for a more respectful, durable and pragmatic way of farming.

> **Beautiful fruit!**
>
> I remember my grandmother always telling me she didn't like her fruit too big. The grapes or strawberries she picked at the shop were always on the smaller side. It's only years later that I understood why she was right.
>
> As you know, salt makes you thirsty. Interestingly enough, fertilizers are chemical salts. They make the plant thirsty. As a response, the plant is going to absorb more water. Consequently, the fruit or vegetable that it will give birth to will be filled with water.
> Even though these fruits and veggies are actually quite poor in nutrients and rich in water, the consumer pays a lot of money for them. Simply because he pays by the weight. Such is the culture of turgescence, of fat fruits. The consumer means well, but he's duped.
> Talented Rhône Valley winemaker Michel Chapoutier advocates flipping the system around: instead of setting prices per pound or per kilogram, he suggests we set them per gram of dry extract. Meaning you only pay for the fruit, not the water.
> In that thrilling new system where we'd only pay for what truly feeds us, we'd realize organic food is actually much cheaper than non-organic food.

The Green Wave

The good news is: a lot of people have come to these same conclusions recently and as a consequence, organic is picking up, both with farmers and with consumers.

> **Organic on the up!**
>
> USA:
> - U.S. sales of organic food and beverages have grown from $1 bn in 1990 to $26.7 bn in 2010.
> - Certified organic cropland acreage between 2002 and 2008 averaged a 15 percent annual growth.
>
> France:
> - 3,600 organic farms in 1995 – 20,600 in 2010.
> - As for wine, 2010 saw 10 times more organic vineyards than 1995, with a doubling of acreage between 2007 and 2010.

Awareness is growing and habits are starting to change. It is a really exciting change to witness and to be a part of[107][108].

The wine industry is also changing fast. Most nicer wineries have all initiated a green turn. Interestingly enough, a number of wineries that farm their land with no pesticides don't even label[109] their wine as organic. Surely because it

---

[107] These encouraging stats ought to be put in perspective: only 3.1% of farmland in France is grown organically, only 7% of French vineyards (estimates by *L'Agence Bio*). In the US, certified organic cropland and pasture accounted for about 0.6% of U.S. total farmland in 2008.

[108] In case you worried about it, in 2007, the FAO stated in a report that *"Organic farming has the potential to satisfy the world's demand in food."*

[109] Instead of labeling organic food as organic (for it is merely food produced normally, or naturally, without toxic chemicals), how about labeling all the other food with a mention that says "Cancer" or "Toxic", just for people to know what they're getting into. Why label what's natural,

might turn off some of their clients, but also frequently because they deem that not using pesticides is just the normal thing to do, and really, nothing to brag about.

So when it comes to wine, organic is definitely a step in the right direction. But truthfully, the most interesting wines I've had were not organic: they were *biodynamic*.

Decode French Wine Bottles

Many signs, labels, charters and groups are meant to help consumers identify wines produced with terroir in mind.

Here are a few examples you might fight on French wine bottles:

AB: organic grapes
Demeter: grapes grown biodynamically
Biodyvin: grapes grown biodynamically

Or, groups like:
"Renaissance des Appellations", "Dynamis", "Nature et Progrès", "Bio cohérence", "Fnivab", "Charte des vins bio d'Alsace"...

Also note expensive **"vin de pays"** or **"vin de table"**: generally a rebellious vigneron that did not abide by the rules of his/her appellation.

---

ancestral and sound, but not what' toxic and full of chemicals?

Biodynamic: Super Organic

> *"Miracles do not happen in contradiction to nature, but only in contradiction to that which is known in nature."*
> St. Augustine

Throughout my career as a sommelier, the more wines I tasted, the more I realized that the ones that resonated the most in me, were usually farmed biodynamically.

So what exactly does biodynamic mean? Well, *bio* means life, *dynamics* means in action: the principles of biodynamics are those of life in action.[110]

Biodynamic teaches us that if a plant is sick, it is first and foremost because its environment is sick, and in particular the soil–diseases being viewed as mere symptoms of a bigger problem. Biodynamic viticulture aims at restoring the life of the soil as well as intensifying the exchanges between the plant and its environment.

---

[110] And as such, they are the exact opposite of so-called "conventional" farming that is fully based on killing, last-scene-of-Scarface style.

> **Organic vs. Biodynamic**
>
> The main measurable difference between vineyards farmed organically or biodynamically lies in the life of the soil. The level of life in the soil is significantly higher with biodynamic, especially deep down[111]. Since a soil full of life facilitates the transmission of the nutrients from the soil to the plant, grapes grown biodynamically capture their terroir more strikingly. Which is of course non-measurable but very easy to experience by simply treating yourself with a bottle of biodynamic wine.

The first time I saw a biodynamic *vigneron* at work was in the Loire valley. I was rather young at the time and not utterly familiar with biodynamic farming. After a few hours of working by his side, it seemed clear to me that he had officially gone *loco*: planning his work based on a calendar of "flower days", "leaf days", "root days" or "fruit days", using preparations bearing the strangest names that seemed right out of some occult spell book (manure-filled cow horn, stinging nettle...), talking about the cosmos and the moon, etc.

But at the end of the day, his wines were so delicious and his vineyard seemed so healthy that I was left with two possibilities: calling him crazy, or calling myself ignorant[112].

---

[111] See the works of the *Institut de recherche pour l'agriculture d'Oberwil* for details or any bottle made by one of the wineries listed above in the coming paragraph.
[112] In case you wondered, I picked option B.

A fancy bunch of crazies

A great number of wineries have ever since adopted biodynamic farming and its cortege of apparent oddities. Including some of the most prestigious wineries in the world: Domaine de la Romanée-Conti [113], the great wines of Joseph Drouhin, M. Chapoutier, or Olivier Leflaive, Domaine Zind-Humbrecht, Château Pontet-Canet, M. Lapierre, Domaine Huet, Dagueneau, Opus One [113], Dominio de Pingus, etc[114].

With much pragmatism, they all accepted to unlearn what they had been taught in school. And they all turned to the option that seemed to bear the best results: biodynamic farming. Said like this, it seems like a rather normal thing to do.

Yet, switching to biodynamic farming takes accepting that some things are still beyond our knowledge[115], and that of our time[116]. It is actually what I find utterly exciting and genuinely inspiring about it: these people that make some of the best wines in the world all accepted the fact that they did not understand everything. They all changed the way they worked and thought. And well, while some of what they do might indeed seem Harry Potterish, it sure does work[117]! Their

---

[113] Partially.
[114] See appendix for a worldwide list of biodynamic wineries.
[115] Despite their utmost expertise in their field.
[116] Or at least that of our time's current body of science, given that biodynamic farming, though not fully explained, is practiced with great results throughout the world.
[117] Is it because of TLC applied to their vineyard or because of the biodynamic recipes? Hard to say. Either way, the differences in soil life between organic and biodynamic soils seem to be a significant indication for the latter.

soil is back to being full of life and their wines taste better than ever before.

> **I'll drink to that!**
>
> The biodynamic movement is just one small glimpse into the incredible amount of knowledge we have not acquired or tapped into yet. If we keep our minds open, and our thirst for knowledge intact, there are formidable perspectives and opportunities out there for generations to come.

Wine Renaissance

The surge of biodynamics today is part of a discrete revolution in the world of wine. The best wineries have or are all converting to organic, and for many of them, at the end of the day, to biodynamic. Simply because the results are striking! And what's fantastic is that they get rewarded not only with healthier soil and better grapes, but consequently by tastier wines as well, which frequently translates into more money in their pocket.

This sure does not go unnoticed with their neighbors. Just like in the seventies, when all the neighbors would successively convert to chemicals, what's happening right now is the exact opposite. We're living in a time of Renaissance for good wine.

I'll drink to that as well!!

Biodynamic & Great Value

Many small vignerons work their vine biodynamically (or lean strongly towards it) and make marvelous wines. Here are some of my favorite ones if you want to keep budget down:

Jacques Broustet in Bordeaux (Château Lamery), Charlotte and Jean-Baptiste Sénat in the Languedoc, Sylvie Spielmann in Alsace, Catherine et Jean-Marie le Bihan in the South-West (Domaine Mouthes le Bihan), Pierre Larmandier in Champagne (Champagne Larmandier-Bernier), François de Chavanes in the Jura (Château de Chavanes), Jean-Claude Lapalu in the Beaujolais, René Mosse in the Loire Valley (Domaine Mosse), Marcel Richaud in the Rhône Valley...

> **The grapes...**
> **Alright, now, let's learn *from* them.**

Junk in the trunk

> *"Any food that requires enhancing by the use of chemical substances should in no way be considered a food."*
> — John H. Tobe

> *"Let thy food be thy medicine."*
> — Hippocrates

We like to think of the food we eat as a constant: an apple today is just like an apple a century ago. Unfortunately, it is not the case: with most of our food today being grown on impoverished soil, it is much poorer in nutrients than it used to be. As Prof. Tim Lang[118] puts it: "you would have to eat eight oranges today to get the same amount of vitamin A your grandparents got from a single orange"[119].

---

[118] Professor at the Centre for Food Policy in London, England.
[119] As a people, we're fed a lot, but nourished insufficiently.

> In France, every single day,
> a child who "eats well" ingests:
>
> - 128 chemical residues
> (81 different chemical)
> - 36 different pesticides
> - 47 different potentially carcinogen substances
>
> Data for non-organic food, bought in supermarkets, following food recommendations from French authorities (5 fruits and veggies a day, half a liter of tap water instead of soda, etc.).
>
> Now imagine what children who eat junk food and processed food put in their system.
>
> It is too soon to evaluate the real effects on public health. But a hint of common sense should suffice to say that at this pace, 80 years of life expectancy seems like a long shot.

Poor land grows poor food. And by eating poor food, not only do we develop deficiencies[120], we also feed our bodies with poisons and toxins three times a day[121]. Consequently, we get sick: in France, we

---

[120] Even if we eat right, we are quite likely to lack key vitamins and minerals: our immune system and our health suffer directly from this evolution. In a clean environment, an exercised human body is a tremendously efficient and complex machine able to respond to aggressions and to maintain good health.

[121] Interestingly enough, several experiments have shown that be they small or big (worms or cows), when they can,

INTO WINE 82

spend more than $4,000 per second on healthcare; in the US, the number grows to $66,000 per second[122].

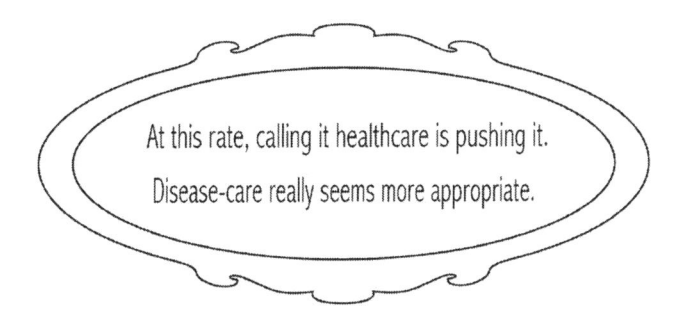

> At this rate, calling it healthcare is pushing it. Disease-care really seems more appropriate.

Over the past decades, the occurrence of cancer [123], Alzheimer's [124], Down's syndrome [125], cardiovascular diseases [126], and diabetes [127] has been soaring in dramatic proportions. Yet, we keep investing[128] in the treatment of the symptoms of

---

animals stay clear of unhealthy food, no matter how good it looks.
[122] In 2008, $2.1 trillion were spent on healthcare in the US. That is 16% of the US GDP. Source: "OECD Health Data", OECD Health Statistics (2010).
[123] In France, between 1980 and 2005, occurrence of cancer has doubled. Source: *Institut National de Veille Sanitaire.*
[124] From 2000 to 2006, deaths related to Alzheimer's increased in the US by 47%. Source: Alzheimer's association
[125] From 1979 to 2003, the prevalence of Down syndrome at birth increased by 31%. Source: CDC.
[126] While they hardly existed in the early 20th century, heart disease is now the leading cause of death in the West.
[127] From 1980 through 2010, the crude prevalence of diagnosed diabetes increased by 176% in the US. Source: CDC.
[128] Evidently, there is no money in good health.

our diseases, rather [129] than genuinely tackling their causes[130].

To that extent, the example of the wine industry over the past few decades is enlightening. The wineries that have persisted with massive spraying of chemicals are generally on their way down, struggling or out of business. The ones that have moved away from that model and switched to organic or biodynamic farming are on their way up, doing great or thriving.

---

[129] Treating of course is key. The problem lies in the "rather" part.
[130] Other factors come into play of course: pollution, lack of exercise, heredity, (vaccines), etc.
[131] Which means stay clear from most junk food and processed food.

Resolutions to build up your health:

- Eat organic and biodynamic fruit and produce as much as possible.
- Eat local: organic is only part of the equation. If your produce is picked thousands of miles away, it was picked too early and will therefore lack the nutrients you need.
- Trust your taste: produce and fruits that taste fantastic usually have all the nutrients you need.
- Supplement your food: pills (vitamins, etc.) are not as good as great food but they will sure help build up your health.
- Stay clear from genetically modified food[131]: usually, GM food requires (or actually creates itself) significant doses of pesticides.
- Grow your own food: it's fun, and the best way to have fresh, delicious, healthy and cheap food (and it can be done inside).
- And of course, a little exercise and some good vino!!

CHAPTER 7

From winemaking to making wine

> **Winemaking...**
> **First, let's learn *about* it.**

From grapes to wine

We completed the first part of the mission: transforming soil, air, water and light into grapes[132]. Stage two is to turn these grapes into wine. That stage, is called winemaking[133].

In short, winemaking covers a few stages: after the harvest, the first one is pressing the grapes in order to obtain grape juice[134]. During the next stage—called fermentation—the sugar of the grape

---

[132] Called *viticulture* in wine jargon.
[133] Or *vinification* in French.
[134] Also called must.

juice will be turned into alcohol. Ageing[135] happens once fermentation is complete[136]: it is the stage where you let your wine sit. After a few months, your wine will be ready to be bottled and drunk.

That's for the (very) general picture.

Qualifying winemaking

I love California. But whenever I travel to California, I always end up in a bit of a culture shock. Wine talks there, whether they emanate from amateurs or professionals, are almost systematically centered on the winemaking (and/or the winemaker). Your typical tour of a Californian winery visit sounds a bit like this:
- *After a first press, we temperature-control our first fermentation in stainless steel vats. Then we do a malolactic fermention. Then we age the wine for 24 months, 50% in new French oak barrels, 50% in one-vintage old barrels. The barrels come from the forest of Tronçais in France. We work with the best barrel-makers in France; they toast our barrels based on the requirements of our winemaker to achieve the right level of oakiness for our wines.*
- *Sorry to interrupt, but... what about your grapes?*
- *Oh, our grapes! Yeah, our grapes. Sorry... Hmmm.. our grapes. Yeah, of course!! Well, we get them from the Santa Rita Hills. Is*

---

[135] Called *élevage* in French, which I find to be a much more adequate—and poetic—term.
[136] Or, more precisely, when it's interrupted by the winemaker. If fermentation were not interrupted, alcohol would turn into acid and what we would end up with is vinegar.

that right Travis, the Merlot comes from Santa Rita, right?

Now, I might be exaggerating a bit here, but in all honesty, not that much. Viticulture is rarely referred to at all[137].

Yet, as much as it's talked about, winemaking always comes second. What comes first as we just went over, is growing these grapes. Saying that having good grapes helps in making good wine is an understatement.

Wine Comments Matrix

"Dude, this wine is…"	Bad terroir	So so terroir	Good terroir	Great terroir
Bad winemaking	Repulsive	Disgusting.	Nasty	Gross
So so winemaking	Not good	OK I guess	Not bad	Pretty good
Good winemaking	Drinkable	Alright	Real nice	Amazing
Great winemaking	Pretty good	Good	Fantastic	Oh. My. Gosh.

In short, here's what you should remember: the potential for quality is created on the vineyard. Transforming that potential into actual quality, that's what winemaking is about.

---

[137] Also because many Californian wineries outsource most of the grape growing: they buy most of their grapes from third parties.

Innovations at the winery

Many wine drinkers love the idea that in Europe, people still crush the grapes with their feet, that the wine is made in the same exact way it was made centuries ago, etc.

However, the wine world is not quite impermeable to time, trends or innovations. As we saw, since World War 2, viticulture has been revolutionized with the introduction of many new chemicals and technologies.[138] Similarly, over the past decades, revolutionizing innovations have been introduced in the field of winemaking.

The activity of making wine has thus greatly changed both in the vineyard and at the winery. And while many grape growers ceased to be attentive farmers, only to become chemical spraying tractor drivers, many winemakers ceased[139] to be humble midwives only to become plastic surgeons.[140]

---

[138] Seeing tractors, over-the-row harvesting tractors and even helicopters (used to spray treatments) on or over vineyards has become quite common. Drip irrigation has also gained ground in a number of wine regions of the world.

[139] Ceased-ish: Back in the ancient days, honey or spices were frequently added to wine to make it more palatable. Most likely because otherwise, it wouldn't taste so good.

[140] In their book *Authentic Wine*, Jamie Good and Sam Harrop claim: "Clark Smith, whose company Vinovation was the leading practitioner of reverse osmosis in the United States, believes that 45 percent of California wines are alcohol adjusted".

Innovations in Winemaking

Introduction of:

Exogenous Yeasts:
yeasts are small 'factories' that (amongst other things) turn sugar into alcohol. They are the key to the fermentation process. The ones you find naturally on the grapes and at the winery are called indigenous yeasts: they are a part of the ecosystem that is specific to that very wine, and as such are a part of its terroir (as long as they have not been killed by fungicides).
Introducing exogenous (not natural) yeasts allows winemakers to have more control over the fermentation process and the resulting aromas in his wine.

Processes aimed at controlling fermentation:
adjunction of enzymes, of bacteria, of nitrogen, of vitamins or of artificial aromatic additives.

Processes designed to increase the concentration of the wine:
reverse osmosis (filtering water off the juice), cryoextraction (freezing the grapes to eliminate more water), sous-vide evaporation...

Processes with the objective of modifying the balance of juices or of the wine:
acidification or de-acidification by man-made molecules.

Terroir-less wines?

The wonderful thing about the innovations mentioned above is that they have permitted the eradication of a vast majority of the common defects that used to be found frequently in wine. In short, wine has never been as good as it is today!

Yet, when you take them one by one, none of these innovations works towards a greater revelation of *terroir* in wine. Rather, they are shortcuts to increase or guarantee the drinkability of wine.

> **Organic winemaking?**
>
> People talk about organic wine a lot but until not very long ago, such a thing did not have any official existence. What consumers bought when they bought organic wine was wine made with organic grapes. Meaning viticulture (grape growing) was regulated, but not winemaking (transforming those grapes into wine).
> In August 2012, "organic wines" were officially (as in legally) born. A new European regulation came to complete the viticultural part of the equation with a new set of winemaking rules. Many deemed this set of rules too permissive: sulfite levels are on their way down[141] but most of the recent winemaking innovations that do not favor the expression of terroir remain fully authorized. This shows that even while there is no genuinely expressing terroir without banning chemical pesticides, it is very possible to go organic without focusing much on terroir.

---

[141] To 100 mg/l for reds (vs. 150 mg/l for non-organic) and 150 mg/l for whites and rosés (vs. 200 mg/l.).

The result in the end for wineries that are not shy about using these new tools: wines that sure don't taste bad, but also, that don't taste that different from one another.

In short, these innovations brought to the market a new type of wine, devoid of much expression of their local *terroir*.

> **Chateau Hilton**
>
> Drinking good wine is hoping to fall in love with it. Paris Hilton may turn many people on (personally she pisses me off). But do you fall in love with Paris Hilton? To fall in love, you need to be able to relate at a deeply personal level. Well, Paris Hilton is our highly engineered wine: these wines may turn us on, they tickle our lower instincts[142], but we don't fall in love. Inversely, terroir wines, by talking to our mind as much as to our palates, offer the possibility of a deeper connection, and ultimately greater satisfaction.

"It's good!"

Let's step in the shoes of the owner of a winery (*feels good, right*?). Most likely, we've spent a lot of money to purchase the winery or to start it. Costs to keep it going are very high too. (S*tarts to feel less good already*?!)

---

[142] Through sugar and alcohol.

> Do you know how to make a small fortune in wine? Start with a big one!

It is a legitimate endeavor to try and make wines that are going to sell. A safe way to reach this objective might be for us to first figure out the style of wine consumers like, and then to try and achieve that style for our wines. Marketing will help us do just that: consumers' focus groups will tell us if people ready to spend $25 on a bottle of Merlot prefer a velvety or astringent texture, heavy oak or gentle vanilla, notes of berry or of cold tobacco, etc.

Next step [143] of course is to go see our winemaker and tell him to make our Merlot taste just the way consumers like it. In short, our wines will be dictated by the market, not the *terroir*.

If wine is music, the soil is the composer and the winemaker is the conductor. For the concert to sound great, it takes the conductor having a very intimate relationship with the part. But it also takes the record company not asking the conductor

---

[143] For the sake of the readability of this book, I chose to place the "Winemaking" chapter before the "Marketing" chapter, which is how it works in all the wineries that make the most interesting wines in the world. Thankfully enough, in all the wineries that make the most enchanting wines in the world, winemaking decisions precede marketing decisions. But truth be told, in a number of wineries, marketing decisions do precede winemaking decisions.

to make Beethoven sound like Snoop Dogg[144] – simply because *"this is what people like these days"*.

Technological wines

All these innovations in the way wine is elaborated made it possible to create and sell highly engineered wines, designed to appeal to the general public's taste. Since as a species, we like sweet and fat, what we got was wines that displayed just that: big, loud, flattering wines. The recipe to achieve them:
- Minimize *terroir* effect in the vineyard through irrigation and use of particular clones and density of plantations.
- Pick grapes as late as possible to maximize grape maturity (and as such, fruitiness, sugar and alcohol levels in the wine).
- Use selected exogenous yeasts to achieve desired aromatic profile.
- Use if need be grape juice concentrate[145] to improve palatability for new wine drinkers.
- Use all necessary winemaking tools to lean towards richness and concentration.
- Use oak to wrap up the aromatic identity and render the texture more supple.

The result being a technological wine, made not to express *terroir* or personality, but to become a branded, consistent product sold in high volumes (think Coca-Cola, Pepsi, etc.). Naturally, those *in-your-face* wines made a killing: in a matter of years, branded wines have not only appeared on the market but also vastly supplanted and driven out

---

[144] Or vice versa.
[145] For big Australian wine brands that shall remain unnamed for instance.

of business tens of thousands of small artisanal wineries.

> **Wine snobberies**
>
> I'm all in favor of readily available easy, cheap, and pleasurable everyday wines[146]. What bugs me more is these highly engineered wines that sell for a fortune. You spend $50+ on a bottle and what you get is a very concentrated blend of winemaking technology and wine marketing BS[147]. Very little soul, very little uniqueness, very little terroir. It is like buying a $20 muffin and thinking that this is what high-flying pastry tastes like.
> This could be considered as the beginning of wine snobbery. "Who cares, right? It tastes "good"". I believe the exact opposite is true: understanding that no muffin is worth $20 is to me where wine snobbery ends.

---

[146] Brands like Jacob's Creek or Concha y Toro for instance are great. The beauty of the affordable everyday wine is that it lures new people into drinking wine. And many of them will end up growing more interested. They are the ones that will pursue wine as a hobby: those who will necessarily end up gaining an interest in *terroir* wines.

[147] The type of wine pinned a while ago as "Parkerized" (after US critic Robert Parker). In reality, although Parker was incredibly influential and some indeed designed their wines to appeal to his tastes (and thus increse the market value of their wines), the so called "parkerization" is primarily due to the generalization of new winemaking tools. For what it's worth, Parker's tastes have changed a great deal over the years; his latest grades favored much more delicate wines than in the nineties.

Resisters

Just like the excesses of "modern" viticulture led to a surge in organic growing, those in the field of winemaking fostered awakening, resistance and opposition as well. A number of winemakers realized that the generalization of these new winemaking tools and techniques led indeed to a homogenization in the styles of wine produced worldwide. In short: more technology, less soul.

Believing that their *terroir* was their strongest asset, these "resisters" harnessed the task of using winemaking not as a way to hide or make-up *terroir*, but instead as a way to reveal it.

How does that translate in terms of winemaking? I always ask the winemakers whose wine I love what their secret is to making such incredible wines, and most share the same answer: *"Really, I don't do much!"*

In order to let the *terroir* speak out, winemakers simply need to do less. If I tried being cheeky, I'd say many winemakers need to become a bit less interested in winemaking and a bit more in making wine[148].

Taste factories

More than half of the flavor components in wine are produced by little factories called yeasts. Choosing the yeasts that are going to be used is therefore one of the most critical decisions[149] of the winemaking process.

---

[148] Pre-requisite of course is to have quality grapes to start with.

So-called "natural" wines

Like any resistance movement[150], that of *terroir* wines has its Che Guevaras. People that just go all the way. In the world of wine, those people would be the ones making so-called *"vins naturels"*.

Naturel here misleadingly [151] refers to the limited adjunction of sulfites[152] to the wine (if any). So while organic refers to viticulture (no pesticides), natural" here [153] refers to the winemaking (low sulfites).[154]

As many, I support an approach less focused on chemicals[155], but when it comes to sulfites (SO2), I much prefer pragmatism to ideology[156]. Simply

---

[149] Two main options: purchase engineered yeast strains, to achieve certain oenological goals (including certain manipulations on the taste of wine), or stick to the yeasts contained on the grapes and at the winery (called indigenous yeasts) and let Nature do her thing. Option two will ensure the most genuine expression of *terroir*.
[150] More or less conscious of its own resistance.
[151] Wine is by no means the result of a "natural" process. Without human intervention, we'd just have vinegar. Which of course would suck.
[152] For more information on what sulfites are and what they, do, please revert to page 169, in the FAQ part of the appendix.
[153] Which is also different from produce or food labeled as "Natural", which doesn't mean anything in most countries, as the use of the word "natural" is not regulated.
[154] It so happens that most of the so-called natural wines are made with grapes grown organically but it is not an obligation, as the term itself is not officially regulated.
[155] And that includes SO2.
[156] And thus also recognize that while producing a wine without SO2 becomes much less tricky if the grapes you harvest are top notch, with high acidity, and sufficient tannin. Leaving the wine on its lees for a while also helps. Other necessary precautions include: good handling at the winery,

put: making a good wine with low SO2 is very tricky.[157]

"Natural" wines have become a big phenomenon in Paris lately. Many wine bars have a clear and vocal "natural"-only approach. The fact that most of these wines are clearly flawed goes vastly unnoticed. It is actually a completely awesome scene to watch unsuspecting hipsters marvel at some wines with huge in-your-face technical defects, simply because they've heard the word "natural".

Oh Silly!!
Why did you bother making good wine?!
You had me at "naturel"!!

I believe that this is only a fad. One most winemakers and experienced drinkers look at with a form of amusement, mocking discreetly all these drinkers[158] caring for whatever is presented to them as "new" and "natural".

That being said, the *vignerons* that possess the technical maestria to make good wines using no to low amounts of SO2 are part of the elite of the profession. Their wines will surprise all and surely enchant some.

---

high quality corks, refrigerated storage and shipping to help minimize the possibility of oxidation or spoilage.
[157] For many, their wines end up showing technical defects such as: oxidation, brettanomyces, and volatile acidity...
[158] If this type of person bothers you, teach them that some stem yeasts that are naturally present in the winery produce H2S or thiols during fermentation. H2S or thiols are sulfurous compounds. Thus, even if a winemaker decides not to add sulfites, he may end up with relatively high levels of sulfites. If the hipster keeps bugging you, tell him that some advocates of sulfite-free wines replace SO2 with ascorbic acid, potassium sorbate or even sterilizing filtrations that durably harm the wine.

My favorites, with no or low SO2:

Rhône: Thierry Allemand, Eric Pfifferling, Jean Delobre (Ferme des 7 lunes), Marcel Richaud

Loire: Joseph Landron, Mark Angeli (Ferme de la Sansonnière), René Mosse, Alexandre Bain, Marc Pesnot, Hervé et Isabelle Villemade, Damien Laureau

Alsace: Mireille et Patrick Meyer

Burgundy: Emmanuel Giboulot

Corsica: Antoine Arena

Bordeaux: Jacques Broustet (Château Lamery), Michel Favard (Château Meylet)

Beaujolais: Yvon Métras, M. Lapierre, Jean Foillard

Champagne: Emmanuel Lassaigne

Languedoc-Roussillon: Pierre Quinonero (Domaine de la Garance), Alain Castex et Ghislaine Magnier (Le Casot des Mailloles), Charlotte et Jean-Baptiste Sénat, Frédéric Palacios (Le Mas de mon Père)

Jura: Pierre Overnoy et Emmanuel Houillon, Jean-François Ganevat

> **Winemaking...**
> **Alright, now, let's learn *from* it.**

The Human Factor.

> *"Making good wine is a skill;*
> *making fine wine is an art".*
> — Robert Mondavi

Making a memorable wine takes being a bit of an artist. And of course having the freedom to express this artistic sense. [159]

Most wine drinkers like to comment on the size of the winery, on the country or the region where it's established, but these elements are quite secondary: what truly matters is the culture that prevails at the winery. Is it one where *terroir* comes first or one where profitability and expectability are the key objectives?[160]

This brings us back to the importance of the human factor in *terroir*. If the owner of a winery decides to subordinate the genuine expression of its *terroir* to that of a style that he knows will sell, he will trigger a chain of decisions to fulfill that objective. The winemaker's role will merely be to execute a marketing decision.

---

[159] This applies to the winemaker, but also to the owner, who might have lost a fair bit of his freedom to his banker.
[160] Granted that *terroir* and profitability are very far from being opposite terms.

A majority of consumers[161] will find most wines made this way "good", but most likely, they'll lack personality. The direct consequence of this pattern is the reign of homogeneity.

> **Noble Wines**
>
> What if instead of good wines, we aimed for "noble" wines? Wines that somehow elevate us.
> Bruno Prats, winemaker and ex-owner of Château Cos d'Estournel, summarized noble wines as "a coming together of terroir and skills. If you miss out on one, you cannot have nobility."
> ... I like that definition.

My experience in the world of wine taught me that when good marketing meets technical skills, we as consumers get "good" stuff. It tastes good, has a pretty label, is convenient and all that, but often we *as human beings* get screwed. This book is also about refusing to be screwed by the takeover of marketing in everything we eat or drink.

Terroir-less wines or food just like *terroir-less* cities, make for a flat, toxic and unexciting little world. One lacking soul or character.

---

[161] The less experienced and discriminant ones.

> **Anthropomorphism?**
>
> My cousin got married in Normandy. For some reason, I deemed it intelligent to go visit a Calvados maker (Calvados is a delicious local apple brandy) the morning of the wedding. After a quick tour, Monsieur Toutain arranged for a tasting of eight different Calvados. After the third one, I realized that his head was shaped just like an apple, like his own beloved apples.
>
> Just like Calvados makers sometimes resemble their apples, or dogs their owners[162], many wines resemble their vigneron[163]. Some wines are gruff, others subtle; some are joyful and some are quiet. And when you look at the person that gave them life, you frequently realize why.
>
> (And in case you wondered: I indeed have rather vague recollections of my cousin's wedding…)

The only way out?

The prevailing winds of our times push companies to produce wherever it is cheap to produce. We've seen this movement take place already for a lot of what we eat, a lot of what we wear, most of the cars we drive, the technology we consume, etc. It seems to be the signature of our times. In this new paradigm, Western countries are now too expensive to produce; their new assigned role is only to consume and to sell "services".

This movement is now at the doors of the wine industry. All conditions are met: global market, technological mastery to elaborate high quantities

---

[162] Or is it the other way around?
[163] Or the key decision maker in a less artisanal winery.

of a given product, large corporations at the top of the food chain and subsequent culture of profits at all cost.

France is lucky because I believe it's gone through the hardest phase already: many producers, seeing their colleagues go down, understood that their best way to stay in business was to make better wines, and non reproducible ones. To achieve that, they put *terroir* back at the center of their reasoning.

In the New World, with wine culture on the up, the understanding of *terroir* is progressing. Some have grown to understand its beauty, but very few have grasped its necessity.

Because let's think for a minute: what's going to happen to all these Australian, Californian or New Zealand wineries tomorrow? What will be left of them when some strategy consultant advises the corporation that owns them to move production of their key brand to China, India, Brazil or Turkey? Because if Turkish wine tastes just like Australian wine but costs much less, do you think people will stick to Australian wine?[164] Do you even think they'll be aware that production has been moved to a different country if the wine and the label remain vastly identical? Did you notice that your favorite French mustard is now produced in China? Does it make a difference to you where Coca-Cola is made?

To me, that's what the future of branded wines is: they'll be made in countries where production is cheap, according to a logic that subordinates Nature, culture and health (of employees and

---

[164] In 1980, Australian wines were a peculiarity in the US (they accounted back then for 0.1% of US wine imports); today they are everywhere (with 25% of US wine imports in 2004) – Source the US wine market: Impact Databank, Review, and Forecast – M. Shanken Communications, 2005.

clients) to the objective of profits for the shareholders.

> **Wine in China Today**
> **Production:**
>
> China is the 5th largest wine producing country in the world.
> Only France, Italy, Spain and Turkey have more vines planted than China.
>
> Surface of vines planted in China (in thousands of acres)*:
> China (1,223 acres)
> which is equivilant to the following combined:
>
> Australia (430) + South Africa (323)
> + New Zealand (91) + Hungary (160)
> + Austria (114) + 3 times Switzerland (37)

*Source: OIV (Organisation Internationale de la Vigne et du Vin) – Note de conjoncture mars 2012

> **Wine in China**
> **Consumption:**
>
> China is the 5th largest wine drinking country in the world.
> Only France, Italy, the USA and Germany consume more wine than China.
> In thousands of hectoliters consumed, we have:
> China (17) =
>
> Australia (5.2) + Portugal (4.5) + Belgium + Luxembourg (3.1) + Greece (2.8) + Denmark + Finland

Wine in China - continued...

The Chinese wine market is growing fast. Between 2005 and 2009, volumes of wine consumed in China doubled*. Yet, over 90% of wines drunk in China are produced in China. The rise in consumption is sustained by the rise of wine imports. Only a small percentage of the Chinese population drinks wine today. But as wine culture is spreading there rapidly, it is easy to understand that the epicenter of the wine world is slowly but surely moving to China.

Do they make good wines?
Well, the level is going up. Many European and Australian consultants and winemakers have been working for Chinese wineries over the past two decades, and that has helped tremendously. A few years back, China produced a lot of bad wines but it's no longer the case. In China at this point, it seems as if nothing's really bad anymore, and nothing truly great yet. But let's make no mistake here, in ten years, there will be, I can guarantee you that, very good wines produced in China, and I can bet you that these bottles may very well become the most expensive ones in the world.

*From 46.9 to 95.9 million cases - source: International Wine and Spirit Research (WISR).

CHAPTER 8

Labels decoded

> **The labels...
> First, let's learn *about* them.**

"Putting an animal name on a bottle of wine will more than double its sales in the United States."
— AC Nielsen Report[165]

Deciphering wine labels

Now that we have completed winemaking, we are ready to bottle our wine. Once the wine is in bottle, all we miss is a nice label.

Though it may seem like mere trifle after all the fancy grape growing and winemaking we've been doing, the label is actually an essential element. One that can easily make or break the destiny of our wine.

---

[165] As quoted in Decanter, March 2006.

INTO WINE

So let me now guide you through the very confusing world of wine labels. Let's take one by one, four of the most frequent mentions you find on a bottle of wine:

1. The petty stuff...

Most wine labels will showcase mandatory mentions like the alcohol content (e.g. 14%), amount of wine in the bottle (e.g. 75cl), the country of origin (e.g. *"produit de France"*), or the year[166] (e.g. 2010) etc. Not the most important!!

2. The winery

One key mention on the label is the name of the winery.

> **Pardon our French**
>
> How to identify the winery:
> - On a bottle of French wine: Château Blablabla, Domaine Blablabla, Clos Blablabla, Mas Blablabla
> - On a bottle of Italian wine: Fattoria Blablabla, Tenuta Blablabla, Cascina Blablabla, Castello Blablabla, Cantine Blablabla
>
> And in all cases, the name of the proprietor (or that of the ancestor[167] of the proprietor).

---

[166] Also called the vintage and which corresponds to the year the grapes were harvested. For more information about the year, please revert to the Appendix.
[167] Or some former proprietor.

Once you have identified the winery on your bottle of European wine, my recommendation is: forget about it! Why? Simply because there are so many of them that the odds that you run across the name of this winery ever again are close to zero.

Country	Number of Wineries [168]
South Africa	580
Australia	1,100
Argentina	690
New Zealand	650
Chile	170
France	**85,000**

Being on the safe side at a restaurant ordering Californian or Australian wine is relatively easy. All it takes is memorizing the names of a dozen wineries you like: a vast majority of quality restaurants will feature the wines from at least one of these wineries.

Unfortunately, this strategy does not work as well for European wines where the number of wineries is much greater, and their size, on average, much smaller[169].

In short: while the winery makes a tremendous difference[170], trying to remember the ones you like

---

[168] Numbers vary and it is often difficult to differentiate amateurs from professionals, as well as growers from actual wineries. In all cases, sources for these figures include: New Zealand Wine Report - Statistical Annual, Wine Institute, Decanter, ZoomVino, SAWIS.

[169] In France for instance, the average winery operates 9 hectares of vine – that's a little over 22 acres— and that includes all the big boys!

[170] As we've seen in the previous chapters.

is not necessarily the right or most practical strategy.

3. The *Cuvée*

A *cuve* in French is a vat. So a *cuvée*[171] is the content of a vat. That wine may correspond to a specific parcel of land where the grapes were grown, to a specific blend, to vines of a specific age range, etc. Each year, a winery makes several wines. Imagine you make three different reds. Well, those are three different *cuvées*[172], and each will bear its own name. The name of the *cuvée* is the one piece of information on your label you should probably worry about the least[173].

So if the winery and the *cuvée* are not that helpful, that leaves us with one final indication on our label, which is the one I would recommend paying the most attention to.

4. The region of origin

The provenance of a wine, as we saw, is central to its identity. On European wine labels, the origin is usually referred to as AOC[174]. It is in my opinion the most helpful indication on a wine

---

[171] The word is also used throughout the English speaking wine world.
[172] One may be made from old vines only, another from your very best *terroir* only and the third one with the rest of the grapes you have.
[173] Or last. Unless you're a complete wine geek. Or unless you fell desperately in love with this very wine.
[174] Also called DOC or DOCG in Italy, DO in Spain. You may also find the new pan-European acronym AOP now.

label; and, when it comes to European wines, the one you should cling to as a reference.

To understand what AOC's are, a quick look at history is enlightening. For centuries, all over Europe, *vignerons* played matchmakers: they worked to find a good lover for each one of their parcels. That lover had to be the perfect grape variety[175] for that given *terroir*. With much vigor and enthusiasm, the lover would penetrate the earth: these unions would give birth to remarkable ~~children~~ wines.

In order to recognize[176] and protect these unique wines, the French came up with the concept of AOC (*Appellation d'Origine Contrôlée*) [177]. Today, 53% of French wines have an AOC[178].

> Champagne, Bordeaux, Sancerre, Pouilly-Fumé, Chateauneuf-du-Pape, Saint-Emilion, Margaux, Bandol, Gevrey Chambertin, Pauillac, Cognac, Armagnac, ~~Jacques Chirac~~*
>
> These well-known names are all AOC's.

*Okay, that one was a joke...

---

[175] Chardonnay, Merlot, Sauvignon Blanc, etc.
[176] When it was established, this mention was intended to help consumers distinguish the wines made with grapes coming from *terroirs* worth expressing (those to which an AOC was granted).
[177] Contrarily to what many people think, the AOC is not a brand but a denomination shared by several producers
[178] Non-AOC wines were traditionally identified in France as vin de pays or vin de table–i.e., table wine. New name for it is IGP (gotta love the poetic contribution of bureaucrats to this world), which stands for *Indication Géographique Protégée*.

So what exactly is an AOC? Let's go letter by letter here:

A: for appellation[179]. *Appeler* means to call in French. So an *"appellation"* is a designation for your wine, i.e., what it's called.

O: for origin. Each AOC is a delimited space or piece of land. You are eligible to get that AOC only if your vineyard is situated within the limits of that particular AOC. This guarantees that your grapes can capture its particular *terroir*.

C: for *contrôlée* (i.e. controlled). Meaning that being from there is not enough: there are a few rules you need to stand by to get your AOC. Rule number one is the grape variety[180], then come other rules (yield, alcohol percentage, sugar level, etc.) that aim at ensuring a form of typicity for the wines coming from that particular AOC.

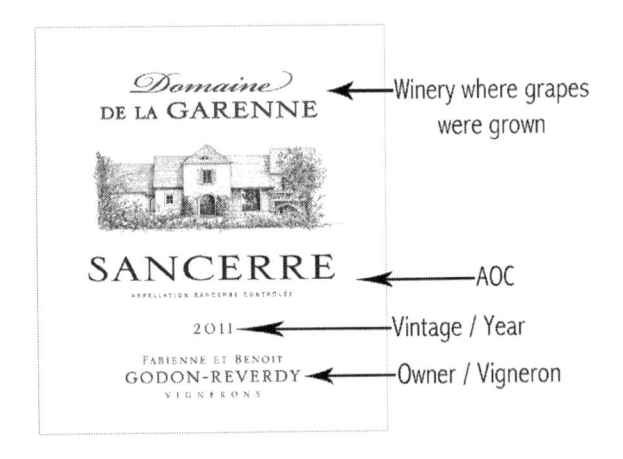

Domaine ←—Winery where grapes
DE LA GARENNE   were grown

SANCERRE ←————AOC
APPELLATION SANCERRE CONTRÔLÉE

2011 ←————Vintage / Year

FABIENNE ET BENOIT
GODON-REVERDY ←————Owner / Vigneron
VIGNERONS

---

[179] And not Appalachian! (I once received an invitation to a tasting with "all the best European Appalachians!")
[180] Or varieties - in the case of blended wines (several grape varieties in it), proportions and varietals are defined: e.g.; minimum of X% merlot, maximum of Y% cabernet-sauvignon, etc.

In the end, you will get your AOC if your grapes come from that particular area and are made in that particular way[181].

AOC's are a wonderful creation, one that has been able to protect and foster the diversity of French wines.

Now as often happens in France—don't ask me why—we push it: we now have close to 500 of them! So while the AOC is clearly the one mention you want to remember when you find a wine you like, trying to memorize them all would be a waste of time. So when it comes to European wines, the general strategy is as follows:

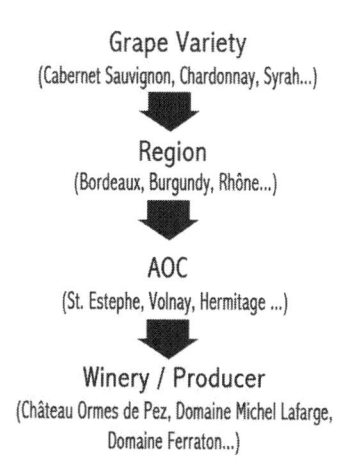

Grape Variety
(Cabernet Sauvignon, Chardonnay, Syrah...)
⬇
Region
(Bordeaux, Burgundy, Rhône...)
⬇
AOC
(St. Estephe, Volnay, Hermitage ...)
⬇
Winery / Producer
(Château Ormes de Pez, Domaine Michel Lafarge, Domaine Ferraton...)

---

[181] In other words, the traditional (i.e. refined through history) way to produce wine or cheese there: AOC's recognize the local historical heritage.

How to Find the European Wine You'll Like

A quick way to gain much more confidence ordering French wine is to know which region grows the type of grapes you like.
As an example, for the main varietals:
Sauvignon Blanc: Loire
Chardonnay: Bourgogne
Riesling: Alsace
Pinot Noir: Bourgogne
Cabernet-Sauvignon: Bordeaux
Merlot: Bordeaux
Syrah/Shiraz: Rhône, Languedoc

Once you know that if you want a good French Cabernet Sauvignon, Bordeaux is the way to go, then you can explore the local AOC's—which are mere subdivisions of the Bordeaux region (Pauillac, Margaux, Saint-Estèphe, Saint-Julien, etc.).

Same reasoning applies to Italy. If you like Sangiovese for instance, well, Tuscany should be your region of choice. Once you know that, then you can explore the local DOC's and see the ones you like best (Chianti, Brunello di Montalcino, etc.).

AOC's outside of France

In Italy, AOC's are called DOC's[182]. They're called DO's in Spain. The new Pan-European acronym AOP [183] has recently been adopted to harmonize it all.

In New World countries, as many wine regions started making better wines, the question of the recognition of their specificity and of their origin came to the table. That is for instance how the "American Viticultural Areas" (AVA's) or the Australian "Geographical Indications" (GI's) came into existence.[184]

On the surface, AVA's like "Napa Valley", "Sonoma Valley" or "Finger Lakes" sure resemble the French AOC. But boy, you don't want to scratch that surface!

A gigantic difference between the system that prevails in Europe and that of the US lies in the fact that only 85% of the grapes used to make the wine labeled with that AVA need to originate from that area. The remaining 15% can come from wherever. This simple piece of regulation is highly understandable from a business standpoint, but it vastly undermines the whole concept of *appellation*.

---

[182] Or DOCG's.

[183] "Controlled" being replaced by "Protected" – sounds familiar huh?!

[184] Oddly enough, the first legally recognized AVA was Augusta for vineyards near the town of Augusta, Missouri (of all places). Napa Valley came right after that.

> **Regulations in question**
>
> European regulations too are being criticized. Over the years, the commercial side of the AOC system has opened the door to many compromises of principles when it comes to the mapping[185] and to the chemicals allowed for AOC wines[186].
> Some vignerons thus decide to break the mold and no longer to abide by the rules of the AOC system. They choose to deliberately 'downgrade' their wines from an administrative standpoint[187]. In France, this happens mostly in wine regions with lesser prestige[188]. As a result, you will find bottles with generic denominations on the label but strong terroir expression in your glass. How to find out for sure? Perks of having a good wine shop!!

In short, you as a client are asked to pay more for a wine that says "Napa Valley" on the label but you do not have the guarantee that all the grapes used in that bottle come from the Napa Valley. So

---

[185] Some covering remarkably different soils and subsoils, (Saint-Chinian, Fitou), other simply too big to make sense except commercially (Corbières, Saint-Joseph), others expanding to follow demand (Champagne)

[186] If an AOC is meant to reflect a *terroir*, why is spraying soil-killing pesticides on an AOC vineyard allowed? How are adjunctions of soil possible? Why are exogenous yeasts tolerated?

[187] To *vins de pays* or *vins de table* (generic table wine), also now called IGP.

[188] Particularly in the Loire or in the Languedoc.

while you keep your end of the bargain by paying more for a unique *terroir*, the other end of the bargain is more uncertain.

> **Percentage of grapes that must come from the origin indicated if a wine label refers to...**
>
> **USA:**
> - An AVA: 85%
> - A county: 75%
> - A state*: 75%
>
> **Australia:**
> - Any origin: 85%
>
> **Chile:**
> - Any origin: 75%
>
> **New Zealand:**
> - Any origin: 75%
>
> **South Africa:**
> - "Wine of origin": 100%
> - Other mention of origin: 75%
>
> **Argentina:**
> Negotiations to regulate the notion of origin have never been conclusive so far.

*This one law may vary in certain states. California for instance imposes 100%.

The very reason why the origin of a wine appears on a wine label in the first place is to claim typicity, or at least a form of superiority over what are considered lesser wine regions. The fact that 15% of the grapes in that wine may come from those lesser regions is not exactly what the consumer signed up for, and not exactly what the winery markets either. So are you getting ripped off in the process? You be the judge.

Having worked in California myself, I'll tell you that it is not uncommon to have truckloads of cheaper grapes from California's Central Valley and even sometimes from South America brought to the wineries to "top off" some of the wines labeled with prestigious Californian AVA's. Of course not all wineries do it, but it is not as rare as any wine lover would like it to be.

Another key difference lies in the fact that that new world "AOC-like" mentions do not specify anything in terms of the grapes that ought to be used or the style of winemaking that should prevail.[189] *Terroirs* in the New World do not come with the lovely luxury of history.[190] Meaning wineries there do not have the how-to manual European ones have. Depending how you look at it, it is both a fantastic asset (more freedom) and a big disadvantage (how to best express that particular *terroir*?).

All in all, the idea here is not to say that New World wines are not as good, but simply to highlight that the *terroir* culture there is far from being as central as it is in say, France or Italy.

---

[189] With the exception of the Canadian VQA system (Vintner's Quality Association).
[190] Most European wine regions can easily boast 30 generations of grape growing experience, while a majority of new world regions only started making wine in significant volumes an odd 30 years ago.

	Sancerre[191]	Barolo[192]	Napa[79]
% of grapes required to come from that area	100%	100%	85%
Grapes varieties allowed by the AOC/DOC/AVA	Sauvignon Blanc	Nebbiolo	Any. Grapes varieties planted include: Cabernet-Sauvignon, Merlot, Pinot Noir, Sangiovese, Zinfandel, Petit Verdot, Cabernet Franc, Malbec, Syrah, Nebbiolo, Petite Syrah, Barbera, Dolcetto, etc.

---

[191] White Sancerre that is (red or rosé Sancerre are more rare and made with the Pinot Noir varietal).
[192] Red wine.

> **The labels...**
> **Alright, now, let's learn *from* them.**

Labeling diversity

In Europe, we love AOC's. We have them for wine, we have them for cheeses, and truly, we have them for everything!

> **AOC's beyond wine**
>
> The French love AOC's.
> France has AOC's not only for wine, but also for cheeses, for cider, for salt, and much more...
>
> In all cases, what is guaranteed is that all the steps of fabrication are done in a given area, following a well-recognized know-how.
>
> For instance, a Comté cheese can only be produced in the Jura region of France, with milk coming from cows that have grazed in the area
> (if they hadn't, their milk would taste different).

Part of the wonderful richness of French or Italian cuisines lay in this shared culture of *terroir* that the AOC system has been able to recognize, preserve and promote.

Who cares?

Champagne is not only the fantastic drink that gives you a buzz faster than still wine[193]. It is also probably the most well-known AOC out there, i.e., a recognized type of sparkling wines originating from the Champagne region, in France. Since AOC's are legally protected [194], other sparkling wines[195] in the world are not allowed to use that name on their label.

Now I understand how many consumers could think, *"Oh whatever, it's bubbly, it's Champagne, it doesn't matter, what's the big deal?!"* It would indeed be much easier for consumers if all whites could be called Chablis, all sparklings Champagne and all reds Chianti.

But what a sad little world would that be? One where all diversity, ambition and cultural heritage would be sacrificed in the name of corporate greed and consumers' laziness? What incentive would there be to make something good, unique and meaningful if it could not be identified as such?

We're close enough in many industries. Wine is one of the only ones left where consumers can still buy from a number of players, including many small ones.

Let's keep this diversity alive: demanding *terroir* is nothing but cultural resistance.

---

[193] As proved by the University of Surrey's Human Psychopharmacology Research Unit (Brits studying scientific drinking, gotta love that!).
[194] More or less permissively so, depending where you are.
[195] For more on the difference between Champagne and Sparkling wines, please see the Appendix.

Read the labels !

There are countless examples of the faux-terroir phenomenon. If you're looking at something coming from Europe, only AOC's, AOP's and IGP's can guarantee origin and production on location, following the traditional production techniques.

In short, if you're at a supermarket and you see a reference to a European origin but without an AOC, an AOP or an IGP, you can be sure they're trying to rip you off.

CHAPTER 9

Beating wine marketing

> **Wine marketing...**
> **First, let's learn *about* it.**

Necessary evil?

Now that we've created our wine, and completed our label, we are yet to market our bottles. This covers several key aspects: setting a price[196], developing (or not) a story around the wine, pitching it (or not) to the press, the critics and the wine competitions, developing (or not) some export markets, etc.

We have spent all this money to make thousands of bottles of wine, now is time to make it back, hopefully with a little profit. Marketing is going to help us achieve just that.

---

[196] Actually, several prices: one for retail, one for importers, one for distributors, one for wine shops, one for bars and restaurants, etc.

I can't stress enough how incredibly different the marketing of wine in Europe and in the New World are. In short, most Europeans suck at marketing wine [197], while most New World wineries are amazing at it. In a country like France, marketing in and of itself has a dreadful reputation [198]. To the general French public, working in marketing will place you right out there, between politicians, drug dealers and child molesters. So in the French psyche, nothing is more distant from the world of wine than that of marketing.

Now, I started a small company myself, so I sure understand the necessity of marketing what we have to sell in our highly competitive[199] and very loud 21st century environment. So at O Chateau, we try to have good marketing[200], simply because we need clients to stay afloat! In short, what I grew to learn is that, contrarily to popular French belief, it is not because you market your product well that your product is not good. Reversely, it is not because your marketing sucks that your product is any good.

This proves very true in the wine world.

Focusing on the message

We all like stories. And good marketing is about telling a good story. Whether it's completely true, sugar coated or full-on BS is almost

---

[197] You will find many counter examples of that phenomenon in Champagne, Bordeaux, Tuscany, Rioja, etc.
[198] Even making money is suspicious - gotta love these Catholic roots.
[199] And, in the case of France, fiscally oppressive too.
[200] For instance, a cunning note that invites you to check out www.o-chateau.com!

irrelevant from a marketing standpoint. What matters is the execution.

In the wine industry, common marketing stories include: the boutique winery blurb, the fifth-generation thingy, the cute label technique, the quirky label strategy, the high-end vino trick, the you-know-what-you're-getting blabla, etc. All pretty deep and meaningful stuff!

> **"This great boutique winery…"**
>
> Most wine drinkers get in a sort of trance when they hear the phrase "boutique winery"[201]. The first question though, is one most men fear to ask themselves: how small is it, really? Most of what are called "boutique wineries" in the New World would be considered large ones in Europe[202]. In any case, the big vs. small dichotomy is quite simplistic and quite far from the reality of things. In France for instance, many "coopératives" would classify as big guys if you look at the volume of wine they produce. Yet, they work with the humblest of grape growers. Just like the small guy isn't necessarily a good guy, the big ones are not necessarily bad at all[203]. What matters is really how they work, not how big they are[204].

---

[201] Similarly, in Europe, most wine drinkers look at wineries that expand with much suspicion.

[202] In France for instance, the average winery operates 9 hectares of vine – that's is a little over 22 acres— and that includes all the big boys!

[203] Au contraire: lately, many have set up practices aiming at fostering better quality in the grapes they got from their *coopérateurs*. The grower becoming paid not only by the weight of grapes he brings to the coop but also based on the

INTO WINE

When it comes to picking wine and cutting through the marketing smokes, bottom line is: two things really matter. First is how the grapes were farmed[205], and second is whether or not you like it. The rest is vastly BS.

---

quality of the grapes and the various operations he achieved to get to that higher quality. Similarly, some *négociants* (wine merchants) will pay more than the market price to get better quality grapes.

[204] That was not intentional – second sex joke is definitely on you.

[205] To that extent, the organic blabla is another marketing trick. But at least you get something out of it: no poisons.

Too much money?

Grands Crus Classés are the aristocracy of Bordeaux wine. The new global wine market has fostered worldwide interest for these highly prestigious wines, thus triggering considerable inflation over the past twenty years.

Yet, as much as these fancy châteaux like to tell you about their terroir, isn't it interesting to learn that 59 out of 61[206] practice neither organic nor biodynamic farming? Bordeaux people will tell you "Organic is good, it's great actually but here in Bordeaux, it's not possible". So they start telling you about "reasonable" or "responsible" viticulture.

With so many small farmers worldwide at bay and only wishing they had the money to move back to "what's right", it is disappointing to see people in the most comfortable of predicaments lacking the courage to engage in these changes, for fear of killing the golden eggs' chick. Lately, amongst serious wine lovers, a subsequent "anti-fancy Bordeaux"[207] movement has been gaining speed.

My tip: save your money, there are plenty of fantastic wines that are better value[208] and plenty of wonderful people with better values, that actually need our support.

---

[206] Château Pontet-Canet in Pauillac, follows the principles of biodynamic farming. Château Lafon-Rochet in Saint-Estèphe is transitioning from organic to biodynamic. Two more prestigious châteaux in Bordeaux are organic: Guiraud in Sauternes and Fonroque in Saint Emilion (Fonroque is biodynamic).

[207] Can't say I disagree with it. When I go to a restaurant, I usually don't even look at the Bordeaux section!! Too broke!

[208] Including in the Bordeaux region, where you do find great lesser known wineries that do a great job with a genuine terroir approach: Châteaux Falfas, Broustet, Lagarette,

Don't forget distribution

An immense majority of wines are sold in supermarkets. If you want to sell your wine in a supermarket, most people anticipate that price will be the main criterion for supermarkets to carry your wine. Actually, wine buyers working for large supermarket chains have shared with me that other elements usually mattered more to them. The main one being volumes[209], meaning how many stores a winery can supply for.

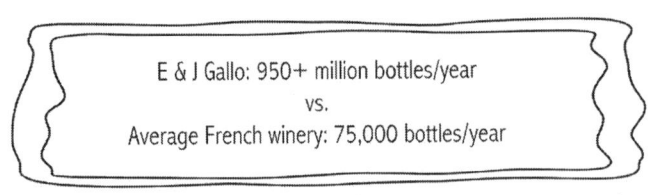

> E & J Gallo: 950+ million bottles/year
> vs.
> Average French winery: 75,000 bottles/year

Sources: Wine Business Monthly, Top 30 US Wine Companies – February 2011 and France AgriMer Infos #169 – August 2010

Clearly, these buyers prefer to limit the number of people they do business with. As a result of this approach, three companies[210] now account for more than half of wine sales in the USA.

Walking the aisles of a supermarket, New World countries like Australia, California, Chile or Argentina come across as very significant wine producers. Yet, when you look at numbers, they are not.

Lamery, Meylet, La Fleur Cailleau, La Grave, Clos Puy Arnaud, Champ des Treilles, etc. See appendix for full list.

[209] Others include provenance, possible mark-up, quality, etc.

[210] E&J Gallo, The Wine Group and Constellation Brands all have extensive portfolios of brands. These three companies account for 51.5% of US wine market shares – Figures for 2011. Source: December 2012 Study by Philip Howard, Michigan State University

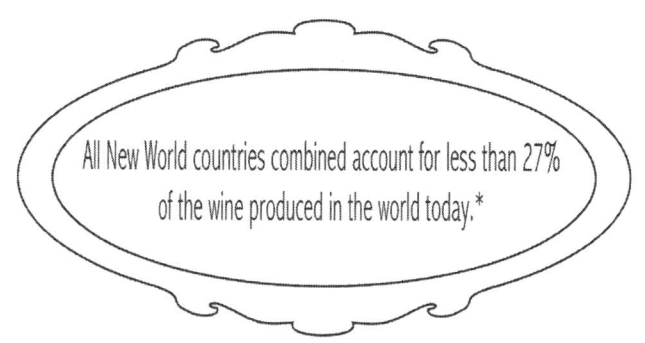

> All New World countries combined account for less than 27% of the wine produced in the world today.*

*Source: Food and Agriculture Organization (FAO) of the United Nations. Data for 2010 – measured in volume of wine produced

New World countries have championed the game of making mass-market wines[211]: branded wines that are fully inspired by a distribution and marketing-driven approach to the business of wine. These are predominantly the wines you'll find in your local supermarket[212]. Meaning if you are interested in *terroir* wines, supermarkets are rarely[213] the right place to go.

The real dichotomy

The world of wine is filled with bogus dichotomies: France vs. California, New World vs. Old World, large wineries vs. small wineries, white vs. red, etc.

The one real split to me, the only one that truly matters is around that notion of *terroir* and what wineries decide to do with it. The split is cultural, and paradigmatic, it is not geographic.

---

[212] In case you needed one more excuse to ditch your local supermarket.
[213] You will find the occasional counter example and in that case, don't hesitate, as prices can be really good.

> **How, not Who**
>
> One of the very best examples of terroir wine I had the opportunity to taste in Australia was at a winery called Clarendon Hills. This winery belongs to E & J Gallo.[214]

If consumers demand more *terroir*, I am confident that more and more wineries, be they small or large, in the Old or the New World, will start making wines that are more expressive of *terroir*.

---

[214] Gallo's management was smart enough to let Roman Bratasiuk (Clarendon Hills' founder and winemaker) do his thing, with his style, his objective, and know-how, even after they bought most of his shares. Funnily enough, when I checked out Clarendon Hills' description on Gallo's website, they did refer to terroir, but they misspelled it!

> **Wine Marketing...**
> **Alright, now, let's learn *from* it.**

Value for money

In the world of wine, marketing efforts are not focused only on selling. They're also directed at selling for a substantial profit. Because let's face it: it does take some serious conditioning to spend 50 dollars for 75cl of fermented grape juice.

The great news is that nowadays, we know how to consistently make good wine; the know-hows and technology have become widely available. Consequently, good wine is not something you should have to pay a lot of money for.

To me, there are two things truly worth paying more for in wine: less chemicals[215] and genuine uniqueness. *Terroir* wines offer both. They give you access to something unique: a unique taste, a unique expression, a unique emotion.

In short: breaking the bank for a wine with no expression of *terroir* is just a huge waste of your money. Good news is: *terroir* wines are not necessarily that expensive. France and Italy for instance offer countless wines that genuinely express their *terroir*, and go for less than 20 dollars.[216]

---

[215] Meaning more work on the vineyard – which will save you a lot of money and sufferings in the long run.
[216] In France, aim for the Languedoc, or the Beaujolais. Find a good wine shop and explore AOCs like Muscadet, Anjou, Bourgueil, Aligoté de Bourgogne, Côtes de Bergerac, "Small" Bordeaux, Gaillac, Côtes chalonnaises, etc ....

Your money's worth

Most wine drinkers in the world reckon that New World wines are quite good value, as opposed to European wines, which are more pricey. My opinion is not that one.
Let me try to explain why:

- Most of the cheaper New World wines (less than $10) are produced in a way that requires significant doses of chemicals. So the wine is cheap, but the long-term implications on our health and the environment may not be.

- For the more expensive tier in the New World (over $15), you usually get good wine. Yet, rarely do they come with much of an expression of terroir. Meaning in the end, what you get is a well-made fruit-forward wine.

But to get that, you don't need to break the bank. Countless wine regions will offer you this style of wine for little money: South Africa, Argentina, Chile, Spain, or Southern France just to name a few. The European tradition prompts you to pay more for wines that give you something you can't find anywhere else. Terroir is what is worth paying for. Because terroir has to do with rarity. Quality these days has almost become the rule of thumb. And it's wonderful. But it means that if you're going to spend some money, you'd better get more than just quality .

Aspirations

> *"Some people think luxury is the opposite of poverty. It is not. It is the opposite of vulgarity."*
> — Coco Channel

Studying wine, I grew to realize that what separates most of us from luxury is generally not money. It's merely our priorities. For truly, is being surrounded with beauty a luxury or a necessity? Is eating healthy food a luxury or a necessity? Is listening to beautiful music a luxury or a necessity?

Inversely: is owning a flat screen TV a luxury or a necessity? Is buying the latest smart phone a luxury or a necessity? Is downloading ringtones a luxury or a necessity? Is treating yourself with a sixth pair of shoes a luxury or a necessity?

The real luxury in our plentiful world is substance. Finding this substance is more accessible than you think. Price is really only one aspect of the notion of luxury. A luxurious wine to me is not an expensive one; it is one with substance, one that reveals its *terroir* with grace.

Now saying that beautiful music, breathtaking views, healthy food and *terroir* wines are not a luxury sounds like the ultimate snobbish thing to say. But I genuinely believe that the exact opposite is true: the logic of *terroir* is not an elitist logic. It is a logic of higher aspirations we all carry inside of us.

INTO WINE

CHAPTER 10

PR: don't trust the hype!

> **Wine PR:**
> **First, now, let's learn *about* it.**

Public Relations

From huge conglomerates lobbying to introduce new laws to small wineries struggling to create a Facebook page[217], the world of wine PR is a very diverse one.

Regardless of their size or computer literacy, what most wine operations have in common is a need for notoriety. If you own a winery, you're after all just one out of hundreds of thousands of wineries that any wine drinker, wine shop owner or restaurateur can buy from. Or hear about.

That is why, just like small thugs need *street cred*, wineries need *wine cred*: qualified people

---

[217] Many of the wineries we work with at O Chateau don't even use emails.

vouching that their wine is legit'. The main channels to achieve wine cred being wine competitions, wine magazines, wine blogs, wine guides, and advertisement. At the center of them all, the so-called wine expert!!

The Wine Expert (capital W, capital E).

The passages from wine drinker to wine snob and from wine snob to wine expert are mostly in the eyes of the beholder: for that, Anglos trust wine certifications[218] while Europeans mostly look at your track record[219].

Amateurs & Professionals

When I post an ad for a job, I usually get applications both from wine professionals and from people who wish to become pros. You'd be surprised how many experienced professionals (wine salesmen, restaurateurs, wine marketing folks, etc.) lack actual wine knowledge. Reversely, many of the people with the most impressive wine knowledge I've ever met were amateurs with a devouring passion.

One of my favorite "Wine Expert" experiences was with a very posh lady that asked to meet with me to talk about her activity as a wine auctioneer. She condescendingly handed me her business card — thick, heavy, devastatingly elegant with underneath her name the irrefutable mention

---

[218] Probably much more than they should.
[219] If you're a professional, that means where you('ve) work(ed). If you're not, that means what your cellar and your bookshelves look like.

"*Experte en Vin*". She decided to sign up for a seminar I was leading "just to see what I do". After 30 minutes, she interrupted me to ask if I would clarify whether Merlot was a region or a grape[220]!

Only human...

The wine cred trick most wineries are after works wonders. A good review or a good grade in a prestigious publication and your sales work will be highly facilitated. This is why I would recommend you take reviews and grades with a certain distance. Yes, my recommendation is not to trust recommendations, thank you.

I have several reasons for that. The first one comes from the conditions of the tasting. Robert Parker[221] himself says it: *"I admit that I gave very good grades to some Australian Shirazes that were superb during the tasting but that I would never serve at my dinner table"*.[222]

Now, when I said conditions, you probably thought bright light, odorless room, perfect silence, etc. In reality, I was mostly referring to tasting dinners in Michelin-starred restaurants, all-inclusive travel packages to come taste at the winery, sample bottles consisting of three cases, etc. Many journalists, critics and bloggers[223] are

---

[220] If you don't know, this joke probably didn't make you laugh. It's OK not to know by the way. Just don't print out a business card saying you're a wine expert. And for the record, Merlot is a grape variety.
[221] Uber guru of wine critics.
[222] Robert Parker –as quoted in Revue des Vins de France- April 2003.
[223] Not all of course.

quite happy to receive the occasional VIP treatment[224] from certain wineries.[225]

I'll plead guilty myself. And I'll make the matter worse: when you get a chance to spend time with some of these *vignerons*, to learn from them, let's face it, you also get to drink in excess with them, which creates a special bond. I'll admit it with much joy: I'm partial to the wines made by people I spent drunken evenings with. I remember a fantastic dinner hosted by one of France's most talented wine characters: wonderful table set up in the middle of one of the world's most prestigious vineyards, private chef, six courses, seven different wines tasted. And at the end of dinner, our host tells us: "I need to show you the vineyard: there is nothing like driving through the vineyard at night, under the moonlight". We proceed to hop in his jeep with a couple of other guests, our host puts the key in the ignition and his CD player starts playing some call to prayer in Arabic[226]. "Listen to this: it is sublime, listen to the spirituality and the intensity in this". Taken by enthusiasm (and generous pours), he blasts his stereo to maximum volume. And here we are, all remarkably drunk, under a full moon, riding in one of the world's greatest vineyards, listening to the most harmonious of Allah Akbar's. How can you remain objective after that?

---

[224] With that being said, a majority of tastings are performed in minimalistic conditions.
[225] The trick works the other way around too: some big names of the wine world—famous critics, a certain (former now) Master of Wine, certain world champion sommeliers—charge wineries hefty sums to "taste" their wines. For a mere 5, 10 or 20,000 dollars, this reputable critic shall publish a review sharing the fantastic emotion he felt tasting that wine. You bet he did!!
[226] Also known as Azaan (clearly, I googled that).

> ### Medals & Awards
>
> Same caution ought to be applied with the well-known medals. First off, simply because they have everything to lose in them, the best wineries never present their wines in those contests. Which is understandable when you know for instance that Charles Shaw (aka "two-buck chuck"), a wine that retails in Trader Joe's for $1.99 won a blind tasting competitions a few years back*. Not exactly good publicity for the other contestants.
>
> While a majority of the wine competitions out there are run and operated according to a respectable process, some are more shady: are the wines really blind tasted? Is the wine poured really the one supposed to correspond to the label? What's the percentage of contestants that end up with a medal? Hard to know.
>
> That being said, a great review, a number of good grades given by different publications, a gold medal obtained even at the most obscure of competitions are always encouraging hints.

*Charles Shaw's 2005 California chardonnay was judged Best Chardonnay from California at the Commercial Wine Competition of the 2007 California Exposition and State Fair. The chardonnay received 98 points, a double gold, with accolades of Best of California and Best of Class. All this for $1.99!

Numbers, schnumbers

> *"What labels me, negates me."*
> — Friedrich Nietzsche

We all spent at least fifteen years of our lives in school, so grades and ratings is something we all get. In wine, that translates into our blind belief that a wine scoring 97 is better than one that scores 92. But if you take a second to think about it: is that really the case?

The answer of course, is no.

> Let's listen to what Antoine de Saint-Exupéry's Little Prince has to say:
>
> *"Grown-ups like numbers. When you tell them about a new friend, they never ask questions about what really matters. They never ask: "What does his voice sound like?" "What games does he like best?" "Does he collect butterflies?"*
> *They ask: "How old is he?" "How many brothers does he have?" "How much does he weigh?" "How much money does his father make?"*
> *Only then do they think they know him. If you tell grown-ups, "I saw a beautiful red brick house, with geraniums at the windows and doves on the roof…" they won't be able to imagine such a house.*
> *You have to tell them, "I saw a house worth a hundred thousand francs." Then they exclaim, "What a pretty house!"…*

How, when and where will this bottle be drunk? Tomorrow? In five years? During dinner? Or watching a game? With a wine lover? Or a novice? With a steak? Or seafood? How well do you know that region? What do you like in general?

We all want readability for our wines—we're so used to it—so rating them seems like a great shortcut to knowing what's good. But we should not forget the limit of that approach: we all have our own tastes and experiences, which drastically affects our perceptions and expectations. I once ran a test myself with some of my university students: I had them blind taste three wines from the Bordeaux area, which retailed respectively for 5, 15 and 30 euros. I asked them to play wine critic and to give them a grade from 50 to 100. For each wine, grades varied from 75 to 98 – one student considering a particular wine awesome, the next deeming it very mediocre. Needless to say, students that gave an awesome grade to the cheapest wine just ran to the store to buy a case of it!

The idea of a grade is seemingly helpful, but it's important not to lose sight of the fact that it is also in a way the negation of what wine is: wine is not measurable. And that is what is so enchanting about it.

Don't be shy!

Whether you're at a wine shop, on a website, at a restaurant, or at a winery, don't be shy: ask, share, tell the person serving you what you like or don't like. Then point out a price range and let them do the work.

A bottle I love might not appeal to you and vice versa. And it's fine. We don't have to all like and drink the same thing!! The secret is simply not to subordinate your own opinion to that of such or such so-called expert. What you want to do instead is put them to work: tell them where you stand and have them to lead the way!

My TV story

In 2011, we filmed the first season of my TV show[227]. The concept was simple: in each episode, I traveled to a different wine region to share about the local wine and food.

We shot most takes twice: once in French and another time in English. But the language was not the only thing that had to be different between the two takes. The French channel airing the show had given strict limitations as per what I could say or do on screen.

And that was fair enough. Their only ambition was to comply with French law. Limitations included minor recommendations like, *"Olivier, it'd be great if you could just not drink wine in front of the camera"*, or *"also, when you're explaining something, you can't be holding a glass!"* or my personal favorite, *"Olivier, sorry, we're gonna have to redo this one– remember, you can't say that the wine is good!"*.

Silly me, drinking wine and saying it's good: huge no go for French censors.

---

[227] If you're interested, it's called *"La Tournée d'Olivier"* in French and *"The Grape Escape"* in English. You'll find plenty of clips and videos of it on www.MisterWineTasting.com

> **Wine PR...**
> **Alright, now, let's learn *from* it.**

The French (anti-) wine propaganda

> *"I think it is a great error to consider a heavy tax on wines as a tax on luxury. On the contrary, it is a tax on the health of our citizens."*
> — *Thomas Jefferson*

Since the seventies, the number of wineries in France has been divided by more than two[228]. While many elements can explain this phenomenon, one of the most staggering ones is the fierce anti-wine propaganda led by the French authorities.

In 1991, French parliament passed a law, which made it illegal to advertise for wine through most main media channels. And in those where it remained possible[229], no mention was to ever be made regarding the fun or pleasure associated with wine.

Even better, since 1991, anytime wine was to be mentioned publicly in France, the person talking was to remind everyone that "excess of alcohol is dangerous for your health".[230] Every single time[231]. Trust me, it adds up and sure has ~~brainwashed~~ pervaded the French's mind. In the

---

[228] Yup, you read correctly, depending on estimates, divided by somewhere between two and three!
[229] The not so influential ones.
[230] Literally: *"L'abus d'alcool est dangereux pour la santé"*.
[231] Don't try that at home, your friends will hate you.

words of charismatic Alsatian winemaker Seppi Landmann, *"since the nineties, the only way to have fun in France now is to scratch your own armpits"*.

Since then, the anti-wine lobby has picked up even more speed. Its track record over the past decade speaks for itself: strong lobbying against online advertising for wine, full-on abstinence[232] recommended to "combat alcoholism"[233], rigged figures, studies and reports fed to the press[234], wine presented as "carcinogenic from the very first glass"[235], logo of the pregnant woman imposed on every French wine label[236]... With friends like France, wine culture surely doesn't need enemies.

So while the rest of the world was growing more fond of a regular and moderate consumption of wine, celebrating its health benefits and its beautiful culture, the French government became the lone ranger of the anti-wine movement.

---

[232] We're talking wine here! Don't get ahead of yourself!!
[233] Recommendation emanating from *"Le directeur général de la Santé"* (literally "Health General director", whatever that means), Didier Houssin, in 2006.
[234] As an example, figures issued by the very official and very public INSEE on French wine consumption do not take into account tourists who come buy and drink wine during their holidays in France (that is 80 million people every year vs. 65 million French people) and inhabitants of bordering countries who cross the border just to fill up their trunks with wine (English, Belgians, German, Luxembourgers, Swiss...). A direct consequence of course is official figures artificially inflated that make the French seem like they drink much more wine than they actually do.
[235] Professor Maraninchi, (2009); heavily quoted in the press.
[236] Amendment requested by the Senator of the *Ile de la Réunion*, Anne-Marie Payet. On that French island situated East of Africa, problems linked to alcoholism and its effects of fetuses have much more to do with excessive rum consumption than with wine.

Consequences of this policy

> *"I never drink wine."*
> — Count Dracula

This policy has had radical consequences. Over the past decades, France vastly ceased to be the country of good food and good wine everywhere. Only to become the fiercely hygienic place of a people that grew to eat poorly and drink seldom. Sounds wonderful, doesn't it?

---

5 wine facts you never suspected about France:

1) Percentage of French women who never drink wine:
45%
2) Percentage of the French population who drink wine every day or almost every day:
21%
3) Average budget spent on a bottle of red wine in France:
$3.8 (i.e. 3€)
4) Percentage of still wines bought in France for less than €6/liter (that's $5.6/btl):
91%
5) Younger French drink three times less wine than their elders.

With the domestic market dwindling, the French wine industry took a big hit: the number of wineries crashed, so did the average consumption as well as the proportion of regular wine drinkers.

But besides these measurable elements, it is a vastly non-measurable one that is the most devastating: and that is the severe depletion of wine culture in France.

This set of new regulations[237] triggered (much to the horror of every upper class Francophile raving about *"the much more reasonable approach to drinking that the French have"*) not only a massive surge in binge drinking habits amongst French youth [238] but also a growing disinterest from wine from most French people.

But why?

"Lee, let me introduce you to Carter's theory of criminal investigation: follow the rich white man".
— Detective James Carter[239]

Most people in the world would agree that wine is a fantastic asset for France, one generating wonders for the country in terms of image, tourism, employment, exports, etc. As such, any person with a hint of common sense[240] would think the French government would stand 200% behind its wine industry. Unfortunately, it is not so[241].

To get to the bottom of the why and the how this could happen, I'm a partisan of checking who

---

[237] That were presented as a way to fight alcoholism, even though at the time the *"Loi Evin"* was passed, it was also aimed at protecting France from other countries' wineries advertising campaigns.
[238] Spirits, and mixers of course.
[239] Chris Tucker addressing Jackie Chan in Rush Hour 2. Indeed, this book *is* going downhill: starts with quotes of Albert Einstein and now we're at Rush Hour 2...
[240] But little knowledge of whom politicians work for.
[241] By the way, if you can think of the last time our Western governments did one thing in favor of the people, I'd be interested.

benefits from the crime: *Cui Bono*? So who benefits from a non-drinking people? Surely people cashing in on their subsequent moroseness.

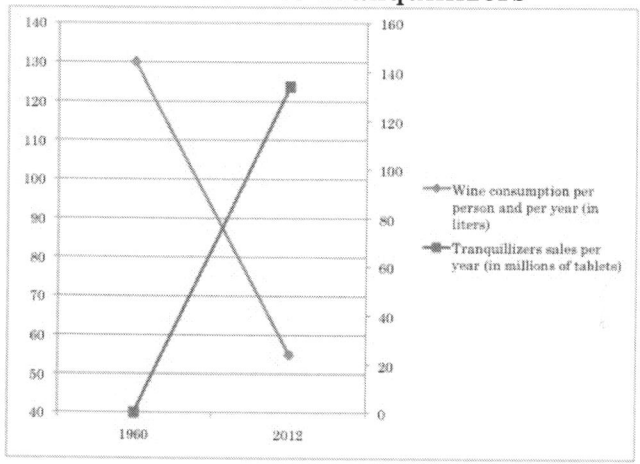

**France:
From Vino[242] to Tranquillizers[243]**

Since 1960, while domestic wine consumption crashed, France moved from consuming 0 to 134 million tablets of tranquilizers a year.[244] With a prevalence of the depression rate that now reaches 10%[245] of the population,[246] and with 20% of the

---

[242] Source of the wine consumption figures: senat.fr – Report called *L'avenir de la viticulture française* (today's actual wine consumption figures in France are most likely lower than the official ones).
[243] Source of the antidepressants figures: see next note
[244] Source: report by AFSSAPS: – *Etat des lieux de la consommation de psychotropes en France* – 2012. Chiffres pour les anxiolytiques et somnifères & IMS Health France – Vente d'antidépresseurs en France
[245] Depending on studies, numbers oscillate somewhere between 5.8 and 11.9%
[246] V. Bellamy "Troubles mentaux et représentations de la santé mentale: premiers résultats de l'enquête Santé mentale

French consuming sleeping pills or antidepressants [247], this new anti-wine nation seems like a pretty sad little place.

Best part about it all: even though this strategy clearly serves private interests, it is generously funded with public money[248]. France spends tens of millions every year to fight its own wine industry.

> **The good sides of the Americanization of France**
>
> When I started getting serious about wine, I would spend a lot of time at trade shows and wine tastings. I was always by far the youngest person out there.
> For two or three years now, I've started to observe that things are changing. More and more youngsters now come to these things.
> One of the key factors to explain this is Hollywood.
> While in France, wine is always presented as toxic and dangerous, US movies and TV shows (thanks to the funds, skills and influence of the Californian wine industry) frequently have their more suave, elegant or sophisticated characters drink wine at some point in the show.
> I can't rejoice enough for this ironic flip-flop of our global world: America bringing back French youth to wine.
> Mister French propagandists: watch and learn!

---

en population générale. *Études et résultats"*, n° 347, Drees, October 2004.

[247] Source: report by AFSSAPS, – Etats des lieux de la consommation de psychotropes en France (2012).

[248] Through hygienist agencies such as: ANPAA (Association nationale de prévention en alcoologie et addictologie), OFDT (Observatoire français des drogues et des toxicomanies); INPES (Institut national de prévention et d'éducation pour la santé) ; MILDT (Mission interministérielle de lutte contre la drogue et la toxicomanie), INCA (Institut national du cancer)

CHAPTER 11

Tasting like a pro

> **Tasting...**
> **First, let's learn *about* it.**

At last!!

From the exploration of our soil to the tricky world of wine PR, it has been quite the journey. But we made it! The bottle is now sitting in front of us. And guess what: we deserve a drink[249].

Since we are utterly civilized people, we are going to pass on the drinking. Instead, we're going to do what proper people do: taste, that is.

---

[249] Great thing about propaganda: once you're aware of it, it no longer works on you!

The glass

I'm not a fussy wine drinker. Like most, I'll be happy to have a great wine in a beautiful wine glass, but I'll genuinely drink anything, out of anything: small plastic cup, large plastic cup, transparent plastic cup, recycled mustard jar, cookie jar, water glass, beer pint, styrofoam cup, I've done it all and still do[250].

Now with that being said, drinking wine in a wine glass is infinitely better[251]. And drinking it in an appropriate wine glass is even better still. Think beautiful girl in a trashy outfit, in a nice dress and on her wedding day. Each family of wine has a specific set of general characteristics that come best revealed in certain glasses. The width of the glass will determine the surface of wine in contact with the air[252]; the shape of the curve will both play with the volatility of the aromas and with the exact place on your tongue the wine will hit first, etc.

---

[250] Not sure what that says about me or my friends!
[251] No plasticky taste, better shape to access the aromas, better ability to observe the wine, etc.
[252] And therefore the amount of oxidation it will be subjected to, translating generally for a wide surface into more generous aromas and softer texture
[253] In French, we have two distinct words: *décanter* and *carafer*

> **Decanting**
>
> There are two purposes to decanting a wine: separating it from the sediment (in the case of older reds), and letting it breathe[252]. When you let your wine breathe (same story when you simply open your wines a few minutes or hours before drinking it), what happens is that you expose your wine to oxygen.
> Oxidation will have two main consequences: the aromas will open up, and the texture (fore reds) will soften.
> Most wines do benefit from being decanted (I would simply not recommend it for 25+ year old reds), so don't be shy about it.
> If you don't have a decanter, opening your wine a couple of hours before (or more in the case of a young, stiff, harsh red) usually does it some good.

Most wine drinkers have heard of the glass for whites, glass for reds distinction. But fewer would push it as far as to have several white and several red glasses, which I can very much understand as these things take room, break easily and don't come in cheap.

At O Chateau, we work with fifteen different sorts of wine glasses. This may sound like utter snobbery, but it makes a world of differences when you offer, like we do, forty wines by the glass. The idea is simply to have a wedding dress for each wine we serve. Tasting the same wine in a regular wine glass vs. in an ideal wine glass is night and day: it is like listening to your favorite song in mono or in stereo[254]. That's of course the type of refinement you could expect from a good wine bar or fine dining restaurant. At home, I'm a believer

---

[254] The same could be said of crystal vs. not crystal. OK, enough of me encouraging Madame to buy expensive stuff.

in a set of 6 for whites, another set of 6 for reds, and maybe a few plastic cups just to play tricks on your wine snob friends!!

The room

As much as the glass, the environment (good lighting, neutral smells) will also have a considerable impact on the perception you may have of your wine. The most crucial aspect in my opinion being temperature of service: serve your wine too cold, and you'll lose a lot of its aromas. Serve it too warm and it'll appear heavy and undefined.

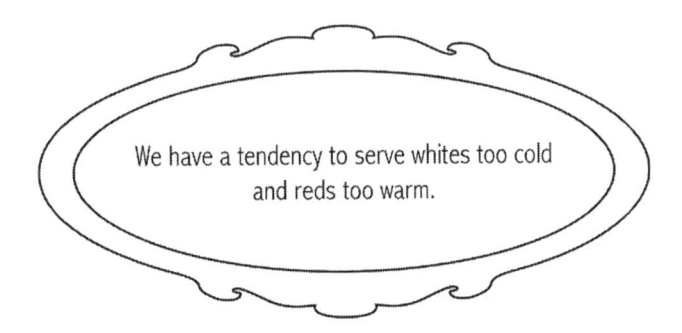

> We have a tendency to serve whites too cold and reds too warm.

The context also matters: if you're having lunch with your boss, the same wine will most likely taste much better if he's promoting you than if he's firing you. Same goes for your health: the only good part about having a cold is the money you may save on wine, as your ability to taste is annihilated!!

These various external elements may enhance or disturb the impression you have when you taste a wine. And you know what: it's all OK! Who wants to live in a white neutral world of oenological perfection anyway?! Bottom line, I prefer an imperfect room with wine than a perfect room without wine.

The (moody) wine

Just like a woman, wine has bad hair days. They come and go with the same apparent randomness. I've experienced many times the same exact bottle tasting quite different one day from the next. It's hard to explain, even harder to accept, but it is just so. Sometimes, the same exact wine is simply not as good.

Just like a woman (again), wine can be tricky. The way you will experience it will be very much influenced by the very components of the wine. For instance, if you try a dry, citrusy Sauvignon Blanc or a sweet, late harvest wine, you'll think that the acidic one is the citrusy one. It is most likely not so[255]. Wine is more than the sum of its parts, and that's also why it's so glorious (just like a woman)[256].

---

[255] Simply because wine is about balance, and high levels of sweetness in a wine require high levels of acidity (hence low pH) to sustain it.
[256] Pathetic recovery, agreed!

INTO WINE

> **Describing wine: the 4-word trap**
>
> Many wine drinkers only use four words to describe wine: dry, sweet, oaky, fruity. And most misuse these terms. The odds that the person saying one of these words and the person hearing it both have the same perception in mind, and that this perception be the one this word is supposed to describe is rather low (trust me, I witness it on a daily basis).
>
> I cannot encourage you enough to set yourself free from these barriers. To best describe a wine, use adjectives you'd use to describe a person: it your wine shy, generous, loud, sensual, rugged, troubled, energetic, charming, rough around the edges, discreet, opulent, austere, tired, masculine, vibrant, etc.

Wine is a fragile little thing. It doesn't like brutality. So be it after bottling or shipping, wine likes some alone time. If you grant him that personal space, it will most likely taste better when you open the bottle.

Wine is also a living thing. We're all familiar with the fact that it can be old, or young. But fewer people realize that it also goes through cycles: periods of time where it will taste great, others where it will seem completely out of it. Maybe you've experienced that "I remember liking it more" feeling. Well, rest assured, it's not necessarily about you. Might just be about him!!

> **Tasting...**
> **Alright, now, let's learn *from* it.**

You are a part of it!!

When you have wine, you are a big part of the equation. You bring everything that is you to the table: your taste, your experience, your expectations, your mood, your hunger, your cold, your stress, etc.

I'll confess this to you now: though my job is to teach about wine, I actually dislike talking about such or such wine. A lot of my students ask me: "So Olivier, this one for instance, what do you think of this one?" I always answer reluctantly because I hate the idea of imposing my opinion and my perception to my students. I want them to trust themselves, to develop their own perception, to define their own taste.

I usually go through the technical analysis, and then proceed to tell them what I really picture the wine as: be it a sweaty lumberjack, a longhaired girl running on the beach, or a Californian cougar with fake boobs. Doing this, I have most people laughing. And deep inside, I feel like I'm doing a good job. For at the end of the day, what matters is never the wine, it's always the moment; it's always the people.

> **Are you a supertaster?**
>
> We're not all equal with our tasting abilities. Half of the population of this Earth is dubbed "medium tasters", 25% "non-tasters", and 25% "super tasters". For each category, there is a different level of taste intensity.
>
> Super tasters have significantly more taste buds than the rest of the population. So, are you one? If so, you probably experience more difficulty than others with bitter food like broccoli, Brussels sprouts, grapefruit, black coffee, etc. You feel the burn of alcohol, the sweetness of sugar, the burn of chili peppers, and the astringency of red wine more than others. Being a supertaster sure sounds fancy, but I'm not sure if it's a blessing or a curse, really!

Just follow your own taste

Our tastes evolve in our lifetime. I'm sure you eat and drink today things that you didn't eat and drink ten years ago. And the interesting part about it is that our palate always evolves towards more refinement. No matter where you are in the world, if you give a child a piece of candy, he'll get excited. Regardless of our food culture, we all like fat and sugar. That's in our genes. Life is about exploring beyond just fat and sugar[257].

When I first started O Chateau, a majority of my American clients loved the big oaky Chardonnays. Today, I find that more and more of them have grown tired of this style of wine. They find it too heavy. And just like any trend, that of oaky Chardonnays is coming to an end.

---

[257] You rarely start loving McDonald's when you turn 60.

It is good to keep in mind that many wine consumers only started drinking wine recently: it only makes sense for them to look first for wines that are easy, comfortable and reassuring. But with experience, most will get tired of technological wines.

That is exactly why I'm very hopeful for the world of wine, and for the future. Simply because as people drink more wine, they get more educated. Their palate gets richer. Perceptions accumulate. The palate becomes more and more knowledgeable, more and more refined. I have no doubt about it: in the years to come, growing numbers of wine drinkers will start valuing *terroir* more. This book is merely an invitation to start.

PART 3

One glass at a time...

CHAPTER 12

Be a Terroirist!

> *"Wine is a professor of taste, and by training us to the practice of inner attention, it is the liberator of the spirit and the illuminator of intelligence."*
> – Paul Claudel

Trans-formations

Wine is a story of transformations: the transformation of soil, air, sunshine and water into grapes, the transformation of grapes into wine, and sometimes the transformation of wine into beauty, love and poetry (or a wild night). At the end of this chain of transformations, there's us.

My journey in wine has been a life-changing experience, one that has transformed me deeply and revolutionized my outlook on the world. Now, I could tell you that thanks to wine, I've learned to slow down, to take the time to enjoy the finer things in life. But honestly, it would be a bunch of bull. No, what I'm referring to here is something deeper, something broader too, something that is at work everyday in my life. If dreadful puns were in order, I'd say that thanks to wine, I now see the world through new glasses[258].

And those glasses make me very hopeful. For this journey taught me not only how broken our system was, but also how we could all fix it all together, one glass of wine at a time.

Terroirist!

The most convenient way to remember the word *terroir* is to learn that people who stand for it are called "*terroirists*". I like the term for it implies discreetly that behind this idea of *terroirism* lays a form of untold resistance, against a world that has gone crazy, a world where we harm our soils, we poison our food, we destroy our health, we threaten our future, and we obliterate our differences.

But this resistance is of the most joyful type. It oozes with good wine, good food, friendship and laughter. Terroirism is about doing the right thing, for yourself and for others, for the environment and for the community.

---

[258] If you're tired of my sense of humor, rest assured, you're almost finished with the book.

Quiz: Are you becoming a terroirist?!

Tick the appropriate boxes

	Yes	No
Are you interested in good food?		
Are you interested in good wine?		
Do you want to be healthy?		
Are you ready to support farmers, wineries and retailers that bring you non-toxic food and wine?		
Do you value differences in local cultures?		
Do you believe in quality over quantity?		
Are you interested in supporting local farmers?		
Are you open to discovering new tastes?		

If you ticked yes more than 5 times, welcome to the club: you're becoming a terroirist. It's time to take action!

If we accept to look at the issues of our world as symptoms, we'll soon realize that the one thing we should be working on is ourselves. Once we turn our back to the immoral and distractive sides of our society, drowsiness immediately dissipates. If each and every one of us resolutely and humbly engaged in small actions that really make a difference, our lives would take different paths. And the combination of all these lives would make for a completely different world.

> **Feelin' good**
>
> A few months ago, as I was walking to the post office to send checks to some of the wineries we work with, I flipped through the twenty or so envelopes. Looking at the charmingly rural addresses scattered throughout France, the realization of the core of who our suppliers are struck me: no huge corporations, no company out of China either. Only small wineries, with mostly independent people making great wine. Through our work, we help small farmers stay in business and prosper. It is not much, as they all have hundreds or thousands of clients, but the great satisfaction I felt was that my actions were in line with my beliefs. I came to realize that, after dozens of drunken parties, and thousands of wine tasting classes, I had managed to stay true to the ambition I first had when I turned down the life in the corporate world: that of not making the world any uglier. This walk to the post office was not meant to be much, but I believe it was the first time I felt pride.

To change the world for the better, all we need to do—all we can do for that matter—is to incarnate our choices into our actions. Putting *terroir* back into the equation of our decisions is a very small effort to make. But it is one that will have considerable effects.

I can attest that it did on my life. I'm hopeful that it will on yours; and that this is the beginning of a wonderful snowball.

Switching paradigms

Solving the considerable challenges we're faced with takes switching paradigms. A simple mental switch to give what truly matters its due place in our lives.

Once we make that decision, all we need to do is replace in our shopping cart what we think to be good by what we know to be right. By changing our consumption habits, it is an entire economy we'll support[259].

> **Typical shopping cart today:**
> Full of things that aren't worth much, made and sold by people who aren't paid much, for a non-memorable consumption, and for the main benefit of a few hundred cynical billionaires. All this while eroding our environment, our health, our cultures and our souls more and more every day.
>
> **Typical shopping cart tomorrow?**
> Full of quality items, made and sold by people who could be proud of it and be paid decently for their work and thus live harmoniously, bought by consumers that will indulge in a more noble form of consumption. All this while nourishing a virtuous interconnected cycle for our environment, our health, our cultures and our souls.

Thanks to wine, I've learned to do just that. I've learned to look beyond what society presents as

---

[259] And in turn, another one we'll deprive of our money.

comfort or luxury, I've learned not to go for the fool's gold.

I now seek what I sense to be genuine, what truly resonates in me, what addresses the man, not the consumer in me. By listening to what's inside, by aiming higher, by choosing to abandon mindless consumption and instead favor interactions, moments, food and wines that elevate us, we are creating a new life for ourselves.

Incidentally, we are also making baby steps towards solving most of the problems of our times.

Tips for more *terroir*

Terroir is one of these subjects you first have to be aware of to be able to embrace it. Consuming *terroir* is about supporting certain people; it's about supporting a certain vision of agriculture and of the world. To support this world, here are some quick day-to-day guidelines:

General rules:
- Buy as little as possible from supermarkets:[260] they have an impressive track record at destroying everything they touch.
- Support your local economy: take part in a CSA, visit your local farmers' market, buy from local specialty stores.
- Buy organic and biodynamic produce as much as possible.

---

[260] You will of course find exceptions, especially in affluent neighborhoods. Overall though, supermarkets have an impressive track record of destroying everything they touch, starting with *terroir*.

- Avoid chains: mom and pop's businesses need your support much more so than big chains.
- Don't get frustrated about the money: remember that paying more usually means supporting people who do the right thing. It also means building up your health and that of your family in the long run. All very much worth it and all in all a small price to pay.

For more *terroir* wines:
- Find a good wine store[261]: just like not all boutique wineries are good, not all wine stores are good either. If you don't have a good shop near you, you'll find plenty of them online that will be happy to ship the good stuff your way.
- Tap into the staff's expertise: talk to the people there, get to know them and have them get to know you (and your tastes). Tell them you want to buy wines that express a sense of *terroir*. Wines with a soul. Wines with character. Use these phrases. They'll see you're not afraid to try what they most likely enjoy too. Your attitude will also encourage them to go dig out more of these wines in the future to keep you excited and coming back.
- Prefer organic or biodynamic wines: use the list in the appendix of this book[262] as well of the wineries listed throughout the book.
- Ask the right questions: here's a set of relevant questions:

---

[261] Good stores frequently recommended on www.MisterWineTasting.Com
[262] Also available on my website: www.oliviermagny.com

- Do they grow their own grapes?
- Is it a single vineyard?
- Is the vineyard irrigated?
- Is it organic or biodynamic?
- Do they use indigenous yeasts?
- What type of yields are we looking at[263]?
- Do they use oak chips[264]?

- <u>Keep an open mind</u>: don't always stick to the same wines; try new ones. The more wines you taste, the more information your palate accumulates, and the more it refines. Sooner or later, this will lead you to fall in love with wines that express *terroir*.
- <u>Use your Smartphone</u> : take pictures of the wines you like, write down the name of the wineries that give you a wow effect. After a few months of doing this, opening up a wine list will become a fun exercise, that will lead to truly ravish you and your friends.

Five major problems *terroir* can resolve

Promoting the culture of *terroir* means contributing to making our world a better place. Let's recap [265] here the various implications of changing the way you consume towards more *terroir*:

1) Pollution and related problems
A product that is expressive of terroir is expressive of its environment. The *terroir* logic leads to taking care of the environment, simply to best express it.

---

[263] High yields are rarely conducive of quality wine.
[264] Rarely compatible with a *terroir* approach as it makes oakiness overpowering.
[265] As seen and detailed in previous chapters

Consequently, more *terroir* means we'd revitalize our soils, diminish air pollution, limit deforestation, reduce the frequency of hurricanes and the scope and implications of climate change.

2) Destruction of local cultures
In so as much as it is its very emanation, a product that expresses *terroir* incarnates, maintains and promotes its culture of origin. Promoting *terroir* allows for people to be proud of their culture and of their work and to live in harmony with their social, cultural and environmental context, everywhere in the world.

3) Death of the rural world
Since it allows farmers to set themselves free from the invisible grip that agro-chemical, food processing and distribution corporations strangle them with, a return to *terroir* would restitute to rural areas the conditions for an enjoyable, durable and prosperous lifestyle.

4) Famine in the South, obesity in the North
By reestablishing the conditions of an agriculture that would be healthy, profitable and compatible to the local context, while promoting the culture of quality, the culture of *terroir* offers each and every individual the chance to eat better and therefore to stay in good health longer.

5) Large scale disenchantment
By reconnecting men and women to their culture, while allowing them to eat and drink better and regain control of their future, the culture of *terroir* is also be that of pride, conviviality and joy. Both local consumers and producers will access a sense of meaning.

There are many reasons to be pessimistic about the future if we don't change anything. But if we do, I believe we can all be a part of an incredibly thrilling wave of change. I'll drink to all the wonderful improvements waiting to happen[266].

The gospel of the good things

> *"Now and then it's good to pause in our pursuit of happiness and just be happy."*
> — Guillaume Apollinaire

When I turned down the corporate life, I was mostly running away from something. After much studying and many wonderful, inspiring encounters and experiences, I can say that I'm now running towards something.

I'm dedicated to the gospel of the good things in life. Simply because I deeply believe that the most simple of pleasures—good food, good wine, good friends—are the only ones that can genuinely sustain us, both as individuals and as a society.

So many people these days struggle with job, family, relationships, health, mortgage; our environment is dying yet we come home to a flat screen TV with 500 TV channels. We live in the illusion of opulence, while the most important things we need and can build our health and our future on are at bay.

Wine taught me that there was an alternative to this generalized consumption high; wine helped me become more aware of this high, and it showed me another way, an exciting, jolly, healthy and delicious wine way. It taught me that putting

---

[266] If I don't stop drinking to things, I'll end up completely plastered by the end of this book.

heart and soul in what we do is not that difficult or hard to achieve; incidentally, *not* putting heart and soul in things is what makes life much more difficult and painful to go through.

Connecting all the wine dots has traced a wonderfully thrilling and exciting path ahead of me. One that helps me add substance, but also spice, and fun to my life. This book is my invitation to you, along this beautiful and inspiring wine way.

Happy Times!

"Penicillin cures but wine makes people happy."
– Sir Alexander Fleming

In the early 2000's, the most popular course at Harvard was the one taught about happiness. It was taught by Dr. Tal Ben-Shahar, who turned it into a book.[267] In this book, he shares with us the necessity to make happiness the "ultimate currency" in our lives: we all make decisions based on criteria such as money, power, fear, image, career, etc. But in the end, what most of us want is none of this: it's happiness. So it is indeed happiness that should be the main guide of our decisions.

By presenting a number of fascinating studies and findings, Ben Shahar risks himself to synthesize the two conditions that seem to lead the most surely to a happy life. The first one is to enjoy the ride. If you don't take pleasure in what you do on a daily basis, it'll be difficult to be happy. But this condition alone is insufficient. It takes the second one as well: and that is purpose. That means spending your time and energy doing things

---

[267] Entitled *Happier*.

that you believe in, to fulfill an objective you can be genuinely proud of, in line with your values. As Ben Shahar puts it: *"A happy person enjoys positive emotions while perceiving her life as purposeful"*.

> **Corporate life anyone?**
>
> By the end of my business school curriculum, I had sensed a form of scam in the jobs and careers I was being offered. I had been an intern for prestigious companies, and worked with and for well-paid and well-dressed people. They all seemed joyless and unhappy. Something seemed wrong about that image. How could they all be so smart if they were all unhappy?
> Instinctively, I made the decision to turn my back to this life and to pursue wine. Ten years later, when I run into some of my business school friends, they earn more money than me, they wear fancy suits (while I wear aprons) but many are just as joyless as their predecessors.
>
> I think I'll stick to my happiness.

The culture of *terroir* means enjoying great food and wine, while contributing to making the world a better place. When you think about it, this means that embracing *terroir* is nothing less than eating and drinking your way to happiness.

Drinking good wine to save the world: can you possibly think of a better plan?

INTO WINE

POSTFACE

"Gastronomy is the reasoned knowledge of everything that refers to humans in that they nourish themselves."
Jean-Anthelme Brillat-Savarin

    I remember learning that about 1600 years ago, Saint Augustine of Hippo distinguished between two kinds of things in the world: those we *use* and those we *enjoy*. Things we *use* aren't good in and of themselves; they are a means to some further end. Things we *enjoy* are worth having for their own sake. They are a joy in themselves. Today, we are very good at *using*. We *use* to reach our goals. But we often seem to fail to really *enjoy* most things, to even know what ought to be truly enjoyed, what's worth making a pause for, making room for.
    Wine keeps teaching me everyday to *enjoy* more. Beautifully enough, by enjoying more, by enjoying the right stuff, I know we can make this world a better place. For us, and for generations to come.
    So to close and synthesize this book, my prayer to you today is simply one word.

Enjoy.

INTO WINE

APPENDIX

PART 1

The 25 wine questions I get asked the most

I compiled here the wine questions clients and students ask the most frequently. Hope you find the answers helpful.

1. What do you think of screw caps?

Screw caps came primarily as a response to the shortcomings of corks[385]. The main perks of having a wine with a screw cap are:
- you know it's not going to be "corked"[386].
- you don't need perfect humidity in your cellar to age the wine[387].
- opening (and reclosing) the bottle is much easier.

---

[385] It's somewhere around 5% of all wines with a cork are corked. There are also varying qualities of corks.
[386] Occasional taint that gives a wet distinct cardboard, wet socks thing to your wine. Sometimes striking, sometimes for discreet.
[387] While a cork could crumble.

- for larger wineries, there are economies of scale when you move to screw caps. [388]
You hear a lot of people moving to screw caps for all these reasons. But screw caps are not perfect either: they can affect the taste of wine[389], they are not as green as corks[390] and with them, you clearly lose some of the beauty, prestige and pleasure associated with the ceremony of opening a bottle of wine.[391]

All in all: from a technical standpoint, no real problem at all; from an experience standpoint, I'd say it very much depends on circumstances and on what you value in the experience of wine drinking.

2. What are sulfites?

Sulfites in wine are Sulfurous Anhydride– SO2.
Where do they come from? They may be of volcanic origin. But they're usually a by-product of petrol.
What are sulfites for? Sulfites are used to stabilize wine and to fight bacteria[392]. They have antiseptic and antioxidant properties. They also

---

[388] And for larger clients too: big restaurant or hotel chains for end up saving on staff costs by saving 30 seconds per bottle opened.
[389] Mainly through a process called reduction (slight smell of rubber).
[390] The cork industry is the reason for the preservation of most oak trees forest. Corks being merely bark of these trees. So tree is taken down to make corks. On the other hand, screw caps are by products of oil.
[391] For these reasons, some wineries are moving back from screw caps to corks. Prestigious South African Klein Constantia is an example of this phenomenon.
[392] As well as some specific type of yeasts

prevent another fermentation from starting once the wine's been bottled. Without sulfites, wine has a hard time resisting heat, light, oxygen (especially whites) and transportation.

Are sulfites bad? No. When sulfites are added, SO2 molecules go clean up toxic yeasts. They go mate with open molecules. Sulfites are somehow necessary to come close these molecules up. The key is to distinguish combined and uncombined SO2. Uncombined SO2 is what may cause headaches, not SO2 in general.

Which dose? The winemaker needs to know the level of saturation of his wine. Experience is key. The more acidic the must [393] is, the smaller the dose should be. For sweet wine, higher doses are required[394]. Also interesting to know that grapes of poor quality require higher levels of SO2.

How can you recognize a wine with high level of sulfites? When you smell it, something might remind you of the smell of a snapped match. In your mouth, the tip of your tongue might be slightly anesthetized. Headaches after the fact also help.

All in all: The problem doesn't lie in sulfites but on the one part on their origin (that should ideally be volcanic) and in their dosage. Both for the wine and for the consumer, the problem is excess of sulfites, not sulfites per se.

---

[393] Grape juice.
[394] SO2 combines with sugar, so it will take higher levels for it to work as an antiseptic for sweet wines.

3. What do you think of oak?

When it comes to aging wine, two options predominate: aging in oak barrels[395] or in stainless steel vats. Oak aging has three main effects on wine:
- Aromas: in your wine, notes of vanilla, smoke, grilled, coffee, toast, leather, ink, clove, spices, liquorice, caramel, etc. usually come straight from the oak.
- Texture: oak aging makes red wines more supple and less astringent[396].
- Oxidation: oak is porous and helps oxygen penetrate the wine, which helps the wine establish itself and develop new aromas.

New barrels have a strong influence on the wine; after one year, the influence is lesser; after three, most of that influence is gone.

Other key aspects in the oak equation: what type of oak, where the oak comes from[397] and how much the barrel makers have toasted it[398].

All in all: I like to consider oak for wine like make-up for women. Sometimes, it's not needed;

---

[395] Different formats exist: la barrique (225 liters), le tonneau (228 liters), le foudre (usually between 5,000 and 20,000 liters).

[396] Tannins from the wood (called ellagitannins) speed up the condensation of tannins from the grapes.

[397] Mostly French (more delicate) or American (a bit less so), but new Russian oak is growing on the market. Oak chips are also a possibility but they are to oak aging what high fructose corn syrup is to sweetness.

[398] The best wineries work hand in hand with barrel makers to achieve the perfect toasting, i.e. the one they want for the barrels that will be in contact with their wines.

used sparingly, it can be quite lovely; when it's the first thing you notice, it's rarely a sign of elegance.

4. What is a good time to harvest?
The general idea is that you want to start picking grapes when you deem that they are ready and that they will be able to make good wine.

This happens usually at the end of summer. The exact date to start picking is up to the person in charge of the vineyard. It also depends on the local conditions: some grape varieties are generally picked earlier, some later; some regions or some vintages offer warm temperatures in the summer that lead the grapes to ripen earlier. *Vignerons* have to juggle with all these elements.

When they think it's getting close to time, while they need to keep an eye of the sky[399], the main criteria they look at are: sugar[400], acidity, and color of the grapes[401]

Some opt for a strictly numerical approach (22 Brix reached, we're a go!), others for a mathematical one (with uncanny formulas like (Brix/TA) or (Brix x pH^2)), many though, particularly in Europe, prefer the old school way and just trust their taste buds: when the grape tastes right, it's time to harvest!

All in all: It's time to pick those grapes when they're ripe, when the team of pickers is ready and when the sun is shining!

---

[399] Rain being a huge no go to pick grapes.
[400] Apprx 17grams of sugar per liter of grape juice gives you 1% of alcohol in your wine.
[401] Measured respectively in Brix, Titratable acidity (TA) and pH.

5. What is your favorite wine country?

France is first in my heart, simply because of the fantastic diversity, general drinkability, and frequent good value. New Zealand is probably my second favorite wine country. Probably because my French palate can very much relate to the freshness of Kiwi wines. But it's fantastic to see the many wonderful wines coming out of everywhere really.

All in all: Vive la France!

6. Are blended wines bad?

No. Blending means using different grapes varieties. Imagine a painter using different colors to make a painting. Using different varietals allows you to play with the different characteristics of each. In France for instance, some regions almost systematically blend (Bordeaux, Champagne), while others almost never do (Loire, Alsace, Bourgogne).

All in all: No problem at all!

7. What is your favorite wine region?

I'd say for reds: the (Northern) Rhône Valley; for whites, it'd be between the Loire Valley and Alsace; and for rosé, Provence or Languedoc. Very French, I must admit!

8. Why does wine smell like apple or strawberry? Do they put strawberries in it?

Many people think that if a wine smells like strawberry, it is because there are (artificial aromas of) strawberries in it or because there was a strawberry field next to that vineyard. Both ideas are untrue. In reality, there are three types of aromas in wine:

-*Primary aromas*: they come from the grape variety. Each variety brings about its own aromatic identity. Sauvignon Blanc is citrusy, Chardonnay more buttery, etc.

-*Secondary aromas*: they come from fermentation. During fermentation, yeasts turn sugar into alcohol but they also transform the aromatic precursors of the grapes into aromatic compounds that are going to give a unique smell to the wine. If a wine smells like strawberry, it is usually because one of these aromatic compounds that appeared during fermentation is close to those found in a strawberry, so it ends up smelling very similar.

- *Tertiary aromas*: they come from the *"élevage"*, i.e. the aging of wine. Once fermentation is complete, wine must be *élevé* (i.e. aged), frequently in oak barrels, but also sometimes in stainless steel, glass or cement vats. Oak aging will add notes of wood, coffee, vanilla, grilled or toasty notes, etc. Once the wine is bottled, it will continue to live and evolve inside the bottle. This will complete its *bouquet*.

All in all: It's all chemistry! The *palette aromatique* of a wine is the unique encounter between aromas coming from these three families.

9. What do you think of investing in wine?

I'm a believer in drinking wine. But if you have money to invest, wine has proven to be a great investment over the past few decades. With the wine market becoming global, more and more collectors and drinkers sought the most prestigious labels. A key element for wine investment is storage: you do need perfect conditions (and you'll need to be able to prove of them at the time of resale).

All in all: if the economy collapses, at least you'll be able to drink your savings and forget the apocalypse.

10. What's the best way to store wine?

You want to store your bottle sideways[402]. Once it is in that position, you don't need to turn the bottle regularly, it is best to leave it in peace. The ideal conditions for storage are those of a cellar: dark, damp (70/80% humidity), quiet[403] and cool[404]. If you don't have a cellar, wine refrigerators are great. If you don't have one, I would recommend to just drink your wine within a few weeks or months of purchase (keeping it in a cool closet). Also: avoid heat at all costs!

All in all: if you can't store your wine properly, just don't buy wines that require aging.

---

[402] To keep the cork moist. This doesn't apply to bottles that come with a screw cap or a synthetic cork.
[403] Simply because movements and vibrations prevent certain molecules from coming together.
[404] And relatively steady temperatures around 50/55°F, 12/16°C.

11. How long can you keep wine once it's been opened?

Once your bottle is opened, it starts getting oxidized. For a few hours, it will benefit the wine[405]. Then, the wine will start going down, only to reach a point where it won't be pleasant any more. This point depends on the wine (usually after 3 or 4 days, there's not much life left in your wine) and on the person drinking it (some people drink their wines two or three weeks after it's been opened and don't have any problem with it). When your wine is passed that turning point, it won't turn to vinegar. It will just feel like a zombie, looks like wine, but clearly missing the spark of it. In that case, time for a good wine sauce!

All in all: Somewhere around 3 or 4 days. You may save a day or two by investing in one of these little pumps that suck the oxygen out of your bottle.

12. How long does a vine last?

The oldest vine in the world is located in Slovenia: it's over 400 years old. Now, vines tend to be considered young from 0 to 20 years old. Just like young humans, those young vines give grapes that are quite acidic, a bit all over the place. Between the age of 20 and 40 years old, vines are considered grown-ups, giving their best potential. After that, vines break easily, the get attacked by fungus more frequently and yields go down. Those are considered old vines. Just like older humans, they

---

[405] Just like when you let a wine breathe, or when you decant it.

offer grapes with maybe less energy and acidity but more depth, and wisdom.

All in all: with these numbers in mind, when you plant a vine, you really plant it for the next generation.

13. What are good temperatures to serve wine?

As I stressed earlier in the book, we have a tendency to serve whites too cold and reds too warm. Whites should be served between 50 and 55°F (10 and 14°C) and reds between 59 and 65°F (15 and 18°C). Richer whites usually benefit from colder temperatures, while richer red are best served closer to room temperature. Champagne can be served colder around 45°F (7°C). The phrase "room temperature" dates back to times where people lived in houses that were much cooler in temperatures than the ones we live in now. I would recommend taking your white out of the fridge a few minutes before you drink it, and maybe reversely put most reds in the fridge for a few minutes a little before drinking them.

All in all: These are just technical guidelines. Go for what you please! Pleasure should be your main guide.

14. What do you think of sparkling wines?

I'm all about good wines, wherever they're from. Counter-intuitively enough though, you'll find much greater diversity in the family of sparkling wines within Europe than throughout the New

World. Primarily because, in Europe, most regions that make sparkling wine use their local grape varieties. In the Veneto area, the Glera varietal is used to make Prosecco; Chenin Blanc is used in the Loire Valley to make sparkling Vouvray, etc. This leads to a great variety in the style of European sparkling wines. In the New World, most wineries that make sparkling wines tend to look at Champagne as the reference[406] and therefore use the same blend (Chardonnay, Pinot Noir, Pinot Meunier) and try to approach (or surpass) the Champagne style and signature.

All in all: Champagne is expensive, so if you find a more affordable alternative to your liking, don't be shy!

15. Why do I get headaches from wine?

The main reason is dehydration (also referred to as... excess!). So make sure you also drink water when you drink wine (can't believe I'm saying this). This is accentuated with very big, overly alcoholic wines. Besides dehydration, other suspects are frequently mentioned: sulfites are the main one, unjustly so (though excessive amounts of sulfites will have an effect on some people), histamines are another one (for reds only). All in all, the hard science lacks. Unless you are alcohol intolerant though, don't settle for wines that give you headaches. A lot of American guests coming to O Chateau are surprised not to get headaches from drinking wine in France while they always get them back home. Don't settle for this type of wine.

---

[406] Many of these wineries are actually owned by Champagne based groups, e.g. Mumm, Domaine Carneros or Domaine Chandon, in the Napa Valley alone.

The headache part clearly indicates unbalances in the wine, sloppy viticulture, or over-the-top winemaking. Or the three combined!

All in all: If you don't get headaches from wine systematically, do turn your back to wines that give you headaches: it's not acceptable. Good wine doesn't give you headaches.

16. What is rosé?

In France[407], rosé is not a mix of white and red as most people imagine [408]. From a technical standpoint, rosé is a light red wine. Meaning you need black grapes to get some color from the skins. Your press these grapes a bit harder and longer than you would for a white wine. So you get a bit of color this way. Then you may or may not subject your juice to a phase called maceration (where you put/leave the skins in contact with the juice). If you do choose to macerate, it's just for a few hours, as opposed to a few days for a red wine. So you extract a bit of color, but not all the way.

All in all: Rosés have a bad reputation but the general quality has gone up tremendously. They're a style of wine in their own right: in France, people now drink more rosé than white[409].

---

[407] Except, potentially, in Champagne.
[408] And as it is allowed in many other countries. Which also leads to these rosés being frequently sweeter.
[409] Granted, it's extremely seasonal drinking - but still!

17. What are tannins?

You know how some red wines have that astringent, drying thing to themselves? You know how sometimes your teeth get red from drinking wine? Well, that is all due to tannins. Tannins are found both in the grapes[410] and in the wood[411] of the oak barrels used to age the wine. They are a key component of red wines. They contribute structure, and give your wine potential to age. Without tannins to respond to the fruit, most reds would simply taste loose and out of place.

All in all: Tannins are a component of red wines. They're good for it, and also good for you.[412]

18. Are all these super expensive bottles worth it?

I'll respond with a question: is the difference in pleasure you get worth the difference in money you put down? For some, spending a lot of money on wine is ridiculous, stressful or frustrating. So for them, the answer is absolutely not. Others save to be able to reach the pleasures of the world's greatest wines, so for them, probably (though not necessarily as some of these expensive wines can be disappointing and underwhelming). For others again, money is not a problem at all, and the peace of mind of knowing they're going for "the good stuff" is what they're after.

---

[410] On the stem and in the seed mostly.
[411] However, they are two different families of tannins.
[412] Gotta love polyphenols.

All in all: If you give me a thousand dollars, you can be sure I won't spend this sum on just one or two bottles. Also (and since there is nothing wrong with a shameless plug), if you're ever in Paris, we offer some of these fancy wines by the glass[413], so everyone can try them at the lowest possible cost, at least once.

19. What does "Brut" mean?

You'll find the mention Brut on Champagne labels. It refers to the amount of sugar in the wine. A Champagne Brut is Champagne with low sugar content[414]. More than 80% of the Champagnes produced are Brut. I would recommend sticking to them for aperitifs, receptions or parties. Paired with dessert, you may opt for Champagne "Sec" or "Demi-sec", i.e. Champagnes with more sugar[415].

All in all: Means the Champagne is dry.

20. Does the little indentation at the bottom of the bottle tell you something about the quality of the wine?

Nope - Urban legend!

21. What is the sediment in the bottle?

First, sediment is not a bad thing. It may result from a wine that has not been filtered, fined or

---

[413] Available at O Chateau, along with about 40 others, covering various styles, origins and price range
[414] Less than 12 grams per liter.
[415] Counter-intuitively enough as Sec in French means dry.

clarified[416] (which is OK), or from a wine that's older. With time, tannins and solid elements in the wine aggregate to create sediment. Another thing you may find in your bottle are small crystals[417] that derive from the tartaric acid contained in the grapes. That is usually the sign of a more traditional—less technological if you will—winemaking[418] style. In both cases, nothing to worry about[419].

All in all: Sediments are mere indications of an older or unfiltered wine. Just decant your wine or pour it gently if you don't care to find sediment in your glass.

22. Is wine meant to be aged?

In the old days, frequently, yes. Nowadays, with the progress in the field of oenology, most wineries make wines that are meant to be drunk young. The general style is more flattering, meaning you don't really need to wait for years for the wine to taste great. The flipside is that this style of winemaking limits the wine's potential for aging[420]. It is actually a mistake some people make: when they

---

[416] Stages in the winemaking process.
[417] Of tartaric acid.
[418] Without cold stabilization and fine filtration that remove most tartrates.
[419] No problem if you happen to swallow some, au contraire, can be an interesting experience.
[420] Wine is about balance. Most flattering wines are unbalanced towards the sugar. Meaning they lack acidity. But acidity (along with tannins) is what the wine needs to age. Consequently, after a few months or years, most flattering wines are going to lack acidity and collapse under the sugar. Tragic destiny!

like a wine, they decide to age it. My recommendation is: do just the opposite. If you like a wine, drink it. Inversely, if you find the wine a bit shy, not quite pleasant, hold on to it, let it sit for a while. If your wine reminds you of one of these teenagers that you know in a few years will be a great, smart and charming person but for now is just this awkward, unfinished, transitioning entity, then that is the type of wine you want to age. Also, pre-requisite for aging is to make sure you have proper storage conditions[421] if you want to age wine. Always keep in mind that the style of your wine will change with time. Most wine drinkers are used to very forward wines; older wines speak in a much softer voice.

All in all: For a vast majority of wine, the answer to this question would be no.

23. What do you think of Californian wine?

Overall: overpriced!![422] But things are starting to change, more and more wineries are experimenting biodynamic growing and starting to favor a more subtle style. I have no doubt most good Californian wines will remain expensive, but hopefully, more and more will soon be worth the money!

24. Does the year matter?

Grapes are harvested each year between the end of summer and the end of fall. Then, for twelve months, the vine is going to work in silence to

---

[421] See previous question for details.
[422] After reading the book, hopefully you know why!

produce new grapes that will be picked the following year. During those twelve months, the vineyard undergoes certain weather conditions. Some years have a rainy spring, others a mild winter, a windy summer, etc. Some years, weather conditions are perfect for the type of grapes planted there. The grapes at the end of the year will be beautiful and most likely, the wine made out of them will taste noticeably better than the wine produced in the same place but with less ideal weather conditions. That year will be considered "a good year".

Differences in vintage style and quality are accentuated in certain countries[423] with greater weather differences from year to year or with regulations preventing viticultural [424] or winemaking[425] tricks to make the wine taste the same from year to year.

Realizing that the year is really about the weather, you may realize that the notion of "good" or "bad" year only works at the scale of a given region.

All in all: Yes, the year definitely matters. My advice to you is: don't worry about it too much. First find out the regions you like, then you can look up which recent years were good for these particular regions[426].

---

[423] I'd say mostly Northern France, Germany, and Northern Italy.
[424] Irrigation for instance is a great tool if you have a very hot or dry year. It is however illegal for AOC wine in France.
[425] For instance, using a percentage of wines from previous vintages to create the new vintage.
[426] How to notice someone who's completely full of it? Anyone telling you: "200x was a great vintage". One element missing there: where? Are we talking New Zealand, South Africa, Sicily, Oregon, etc? Are we talking Tuscany, Burgundy, etc.

25. Is wine really good for you?

There are many health benefits associated to a regular and moderate consumption of wine:
- Red wine helps lower the incidence of heart attacks by cleaning up blood vessels, thanks to its tannins.
- Wine helps fight bad cholesterol by favoring its hepatic catabolism.
- Wine helps lower the risk of stomach ulcers by protecting the intestines' mucous against heavy metals and carcinogen substances.
- Wine has antiseptic properties: phenol acids (in whites and reds) are active against pneumococcus, streptococcus and staphylococcus; anthocyans (in reds only) act against salmonella and colibacilles.
- Red wine helps prevents fat cells from developing in your system (thanks to a lovely compound called resveratrol[427]).
- And last but not least: wine helps improve mental well-being by allowing wine drinkers to relax, let go, abandon themselves, flirt, love and be more convivial.

All in all: Big yes! As long as you stick to a moderate drinking (2 glasses per day for women, 3 for men), you're doing your health a favor by drinking wine[428].

---

[427] Which is being studied but of which many studies already seem to suggest that it may help buffer the aging process, and combat cancer and neurodegenerative diseases.
[428] *Terroir* wine that is of course!!

PART 2

List of biodynamic wineries worldwide

To help you explore the great world of *terroir* wines, I put together a list of wineries implementing biodynamic practices on their vineyard (or at least on part of it). Please note that this list is not comprehensive. Apologies in advance for those I missed[429] (it's a big world out there).

FRANCE

Alsace
Sylvie Spielmann, Laurent Barth, François Baur, Bott-Geyl, Jean Becker (partially), Léon Boesch, Barmes-Buecher, Bott-Geyl, Vignoble Klur Clément, Marcel Deiss, Dirler-Cadé, André Durrmann, Eblin-Fuchs, Geschickt Frédéric, Charles & Dominique Frey, Pierre Frick, Luc Faller, Patrick Meyer, Vincent Fleith, Geschickt, Jean Ginglinger, Remy Gresser, G. Humbrecht & Fils, Josmeyer, Marc Kreydenweiss, Albert Mann,

---

[429] If you think you should appear on this list, please don't hesitate to contact me: olivier.magny.contact@gmail.com

Eugène Meyer, Mittnacht, Ostertag, Rolly-Gassmann, Schaetzel, Marc Tempé, Domaine Weinbach, Domaine Zind Humbrecht, Valentin Zusslin, Trapet Alsace, Domaine Léon Besch, Kuentz bas, Vignoble des Deux Lunes

Beaujolais
Domaine Debize, Domaine Christian Ducroux, M. Lapierre, Les Marcellins, Domaine de la Fully, Bernard Valette, Michel Guignier, Domaine du Chardon Bleu

Bordeaux
Domaine de l'A (partially), Château Jacques Blanc, Castel Vieilh la Salle, Château La Chapelle Maillard, Château Falfas, Château La Tour Figeac, Château Fonroque (partially), Château Lagarette, Château La Grave, Château La Grolet, Château Peybonhomme, Château la Maison Blanche (partially), Château Fougas, Château Les Mangons, Château Meylet, Château Morlan-Tuilière, Château Moulin du Cadet, Château Pontet-Canet, Château le Puy, Château des Rochers Bellevue, Château du Champ des Treilles, Domaine du Rousset Peyraguey, Clos Puy Arnaud, Château Climens, François Decombe, Moulin du Cadet, Canon Saint Michel, Château du Chastelet, Château Vieux Pourret, Château Rochers Bellevue, Château des Rochers, Château Lamery, Château Fourton la Garenne, Morlan-Tullière

Burgundy
Domaine d'Auvenay, Domaine Arlaud, Domaine de L'Arlot, Domaine Comte Armand, Daniel Barraud, Dom. de la Boissonneuse (partially), Domaine de la Cadette, Chandon de Briailles, Domaine Bruno Clavelier, Dominique Cornin, Dominique & Catherine Derain, Daniel Barraud, Domaine Dujac (partially), Domaine des Epeneaux, Les

Faverelles, Domaine Emmanuel Giboulot, Jean Grivot, Domaine Henri Gouges, Domaine Guillemot-Michel, Domaine du Val de Saône, Thierry Guyot, Domaine Jeandau, Domaine Michel Lafarge, Héritiers du Comte Lafon, Domaine Leflaive, Domaine Leroy, Joseph Drouhin, Sylvain Loichet, Frédéric Rossignol, Domaine Marquis d'Angerville, Domaine Montchovet, Domaine Huber-Verdereau, Domaine Lafarge, Domaine Ballorin & Fils, Les Champs de l'Abbaye, Château de la Maltroye, Didier Montchovet, Château de Monthelie, Pierre Morey, Jacques-Frederick Mugnier, Jean-Claude Rateau, Domaine d'Auvenay, Domaine Roblet-Monnot (partially), Domaine de la Romanée Conti, Rossingol-Trapet, Guy Roulot, La Soufrandière (partially), Olivier Guyot, Jean-Louis Trapet, Rossignol-Trapet, Guy Bussière, Céline et Laurent Tripoz, Cécile Tremblay (partially), Catherien & Dominique Derain, Domaine des Vignes du Maynes, Domaine de la Vougeraie, Vincent Dauvissat (partially), Catherine Moreau, JM Brocard (partially), Comte Liger Belair, Céline et Laurent Tripoz, Vignes du Maynes, SCEA de quinatine, Château de Lavernette, Philippe Garrey

Champagne
Françoise Bedel, Bérèche (partially), Raymond Boulard partially), Boulard Fils & Fille, Fleury, Gautherot, Larmandier-Bernier, Leclapart, Leclerc Briant, Bruno Michel *(Cuvée Rebelle),* Franck Pascal, Prévost, Réaut-Noirot, Erik Schrieber, Jacques Selosse, Erick de Sousa, Alain Reaut, Raymond-Boulard (partially), Dufour (partially), Erick Schreiber, Thierry Hubscwerlin

Corsica
Domaine Comte Abbatucci, Domaine Antoine Arena, Domaine Pero Longo

Jura/Savoie
Château de Chavannes, Dominique Dumont, Belluard Fils, Domaine Monnier, Gillez Berlioz, Domaine Pignier, Domaine Prieuré Saint Christophe, André et Mireille Tissot, Domaine de la Pinte, Cellier des Chartreux, Stéphane Tissot, Fabrice Closset, Domaine des Ardoisières

Languedoc-Roussillon
Domaine Léon Barral, Domaine Beauthorey, Domaine de Bila-Haul, Le Casot de Mailloles, Domaine Cazes, Clos du Rouge Gorge, Domaine de Combebelle, Domaine de Fontedicto, French Rabbit, Domaine Gauby, Zélige-Caravent, Le Petit Domaine de Gimios, Mas d'Alezon, La Grange de Quatre Sous (partially), Joliette (partially), Laguerre, Domaine de Malaïgue (partially), Domaine Maris, Mas Conscience, Mas des Caprices, Domaine Grand Lauze, Marfée, Domaine Matassa (partially), Domaine du Montahuc, La Réserve d'O, Mas Foulaquier, Zelige-Caravent, Domaine Turner-Pageot, Domaine Malavieille, Domaine de Chamans, Domaine de Ferrals, Causses Marines, Domaine Pechigo, Domaine des Perrières, Domaine Olivier Pithon, Domaine St. Julien, Le Soula, Matassa, Terres des Chardons, Domaine du Traginer, Les Grimaudes, Clos de l'Anhel (partially), Domaine Nivet Galinier

Loire
Catherine et Pierre Breton, Clos de la Briderie, Alexandre Bain, Clos Roche Blanche (partially), Château de La Bonneliere, Eric Bordelet, Guy Bossard, Laurent Chatenay, Domaine Les

Chesnaies, François Chidaine, Domaine du Closel, Domaine de Château Gaillard, Clos de la Coulée de Serrant, Domaine Julien Courtois, Château de la Roche, Château de Plaisance, Domaine des Rouet, Vincent Gaudry, Fabrice Gasnier, Philippe Gilbert, Oliver Cousin, Domaine Dagueneau, Domaine Philippe Delesvaux, Stéphane Bernaudeau, Domaine de Bellivière, Château de Bois-Brinçon, Les Cailloux du Paradis, Domaine de l'Ecu, Domaine Filliatreau, Patrick Beaudoin, Clos Château Gaillard, Clos de la Briderie, Domaine de la Garrelière, Tour Grise, Domaine des Huards, Huët, Domaine de Juchepie, Domaine des Maisons Brûlées, Domaine de la Louvetrie, Domaine Mosse, Domaine de Pontcher, Puzelat (partially), Domaine des Roches Neuves, Clos Rougeard, Domaine des Sablonnettes, Domaine St. Nicholas, Ferme de la Sansonnière, Silce de Quincy, Château de Suronde, Château Tour Grise, Domaine Vacheron (partially), Vigneau Chevreau, Joseph Landron, Domaine Fouassier, Domaine Les Maisons Rouges, Domaine des Maisons Brûlées, Domaine les Grandes Vignes, Clos de Nell, Domaine de Montrieux, La Moussière (A. Mellot), Guy Bossard

Rhône
Domaine André, Château de Bastet, M. Chapoutier (partially), Clos du Caveau, Domaine du Coulet, Domaine Duseigneur, Stéphane Othéguy, Domaine des Estubiers, Domaine Ferraton, Domaine de Graillefiot, Domaine Guillemot-Michel, Clos du Joncuas, Clos du Caveau, Domaine les Aphillanthes, La Ferme des Sept Lunes, Domaine de La Grande Bellane, Domaine de Marcoux, Domaine Monier, Domaine Montirius, Domaine Patrick Pélisson, Domaine Saint Apollinaire, Domaine Eric Saurel, Domaine de Villeneuve, Domaine Viret, Mas de Vinobre, Le Sang des

Cailloux, Domaien Vallot, Domaine Achard Vincent, Balazu des Vaussières, Château de Bastet, Domaine de la Vieille Julienne, Domaine Saint-Apollinaire, Domaine Roche-Audran, Domaine Beaurenard, Domaine de la Cabotte, Domaine du Faucon Doré, Domaine Gourt de Mautens, Domaine de Fontvert.

Provence
Domaine des Béates, Château La Canorgue (partially), Domaine des Fouques, Domaine Hauvette, Château Romanin, Château de Roquefort, Domaine de Lauzières, Château Sainte-Anne, Domaine Saint Estève, Domaine La Tour de Vidaux, Clos Saint-Vincent, Domaine de Trevallon, Château Mentone, Château Gasqui, Dupéré-Barrera (Domaine du Clos de la Procure)

South-West
Château Bouscassé, Mas del Périé, Domaine Le Bouscas, Domaine de Lafage, Château Laroque, Grande Maison, Château Montus, Château Lacapelle Cabanac, Château Vent d'Autan, Domaine du Petit Malromé, Château Haut-Garrigue, Château du Grand Roc, Domaine de Souch, Domaine des Savarines, Domaine Bellauc, Clos Marie Louise, Château de Mayragues, Domaine de Gineste, Château Jonc Blanc

Armagnac/Cognac
Domaine de Saoubis, David Ramnoux.

ITALY

Abruzzi
Antonio Di Battista, Emidio Pepe, Olearia Vinicola Orsogna

Alto Adige-Trentino
Foradori, J. Hofstätter (partially), Kellerei Kaltern, Alois Lageder (partially), Tenute Loacker

Basilicata
Cantine del Notaio

Campania
Ocone

Emilia Romagna
La Collina, Cà Colombera – Dimola, Folicello, Paolo Francesconi, Camillo Donati, Tenuta Mara, Vigneto San Vito

Friuli/Venezia Giulia
Bressan, La Castellada, Damijan, Domaine Borc Dodon (Marc Mntanar), Josko Gravner, Radikon, Vadopivec

Lazio
Cristina Menicocci, La Visciola

Liguria
Selvadoce

Lombardia
Fattoria Mondo Antico

Marche
Fattoria San Lorenzo

Piedmont
Cascina degli Ulivi, Cascina Corte (partially), Ël Mat di Gaiero Giuseppe, Hilberg-Pasquero, Teobaldo Cappellano, Nuova Cappellata, Scagiola (partially), Trinchero, La Raia, I tre poggi,

Giordano Lombardo, Casa Wallace, Auriel, Carussin, San Fereolo

Puglia
Cefalicchio, Leone de Castris

Sardinia
Tenute Dettori

Sicily
C.O.S., Do Zenner, Gulfi Ramada, Abbazia Santa Anastasia

Tuscany
Castello di Argiano, Fattoria di Bacchereto, La Busattina, Caiarossa, Casale, Fattoria Castellina, Casina di Cornia, Duemani, Tenuta di Ghizzano, Corte Pavone (partially), Cosimo Maria Masini, Fattoria Cerreto Libri, Fattoria di Bacchereto, Massavecchia, Il Paradiso di Manfredi, Monte Bernardi, Montesecondo, Tenuta Migliavacca, Querciabella (partially), Castello dei Rampolla, Riecine (partially), San Giuseppe, Stella di Campalto, Fattoria La Torre, Poggio Trevvalle, Tenuta di Valgiano, Roberto Moretti, Fornace Prima, Ampeleia, Fattoria Montanine, Poggiosecco, Campinuovi, Colombaia, Fabbrica di San Martino, Pian dell'Orino, Podere Concori, Podere La Cerreta, Poggio Trevvalle, San Polino,

Umbria
Paolo Bea

Veneto
La Biancara, Castello di Lispida, Cascina La Pertica, Perlage "Col di Manza", Masiero

INTO WINE

SPAIN

Dominio de Atauta, Albet i Noya, Descendientes de J. Palacios, Mas Estela, Do Ferreiro, R. López de Heredia (partially), Clos Martinet, Alvaro Palacios, Dominio de Pingus, Ponce, Compania de Vinos Telmo Rodriguez, Viña Sastre Roble (partially)

SLOVENIA

Severin Erzertic, Movia, Urbajs

AUSTRIA

Geyerhof, Hirsch, Loimer, Nigl, Nikolaihof, Meinklang, Michlits, Willi Opitz, Bernard Ott, Schönberger, Sepp-Moser, Söllner, Wimmer-Czerny

GERMANY

Bürklin-Wolf, Weingut Eymann, Weingut Fuchs-Jacobus, Gysler, Weingut Hahnmühle, Freiherr Heyl zu Herrnsheim, Sybille Kuntz, Weingut Sander, Weingut Trossen, Schloss Wallhaüsen, Weingut Wittmann, Weingut Im Zwölberich

HUNGARY

Weninger

SWITZERLAND

Domaine de Beudon, Azienda Biodinamica Cà di Ciser, Liesch-Hiestand, Domaine de la Colombe

PORTUGAL

Quinta de Covela, Vale Pequeno

CHILE

Antiyal, Emiliana Winery, Casa Lapostolle (partially), Matetic, Seña (partially), Viñedos Organicos Emiliana (VOE)

ARGENTINA

Achaval Ferrer, Alpamanta, Bodega Colomé (partially), Finca Cobos, Fabril Alto Verde, Bodegas Chacra, Bodega Noemia de Patagonia, Bodegas Krontiras (partially)

SOUTH AFRICA

Reyneke Wines, Rozendal Farm, Schonenberg Wines, The Observatory Topaz, Tulbagh Mountain Vineyards

USA

Napa
Araujo, Black Sears, Ehlers Estate, Frog's Leap (partially), Grgich Hills, Joseph Phelps (partially), Opus One (partially), Quintessa, Robert Sinskey, Viader (partially)

Sonoma/Dry Creek[430]
Baker Lane (partially), Benziger (partially), Bucklin (partially), B Vineyards & Habitat (partially), Bjornstad, Ceritas, Coturri Winery, De Loach (partially), DuMoL (partially), Kamen, Littorai (partially), Lutea Wine Cellars (partially), Montemaggiore, Pax, JPV Freestone, Porter-Bass, Porter Creek (partially), Preston (partially), Quivira, Small Vines (partially), Unti, Verge (partially), Wild Hog, Tandem, Sky Saddle, Radio-Coteau, Truett Hurst (partially)

Central-Coast[431]
Ambyth Estate, Ampelos Cellars, Arcadian, Beckman Vineyards, Blair Fox, Bonny Doon (partially), Carmody McKnight, Demetria, Dover Canyon, Hartley-Ostini Hitching Post, Kenneth-Crawford, Ethan Lindquest, Margerum, Parr Selections, Presidio, Qupé, Rhys (partially), Samsara

Mendocino/Lake County/North Coast
Bonterra, Ceàgo, Paul Dolan Vineyards, Frey Vineyards(partially), Golden Vineyards, Jeriko Estates & Vineyards (partially), Martella Wines, Masut, Mendocino Farms, Patianna, Saracina, Topel, Dark Horse

Sierra Foothills
Clos Saron (partially), La Clarine, Renaissance (partially)

---

[430] Several of these wineries use grapes grown by Porter Bass and Harms Vineyards.
[431] Several of these wineries use grapes grown by Purisima Moutain Vineyard.

Oregon[432]
Antica Terra (partially), Beaux Frères, Montinore Estate, Belle Pente (partially), Bergström (partially), Brick House, Cooper Mountain, Cowhorn, de Lancellotti, Evesham Wood, Lemelson, Maysara Winery, Resnonance Vineyard, Rex Hill (partially), Sineann, Sokol Blosser

Washington
Cayuse Vineyards, Hedges Family Estate (partially), Pacific Rim)

New York State
Shinn Estate Vineyards (partially), Silver Thread Vineyard, Herman J. Weimer (partially)

Colorado
Jack Rabbit Hill

Virginia
Château O'Brien

Illinois
Famous Fossil Winery

CANADA

Okanagan
Blue Mountain (partially)

Niagara
Southbrook Vineyards (partially)

---

[432] Several of these wineries use grapes grown by Resonance or Momtazi Vineyards.

AUSTRALIA

Hunter Valley - New South Wales
Botobolar Vineyard, Krinklewood Vineyard, Lark Hill Winery, Lowe Family (partially), Macquariedale Estate, Organic One, Retief Wines, Rosnay Organic Wines, Cassegrain Wines (partially), Cumulus Wines (partially), Milldale Estate (partially), Tamburlaine, Walden Woods Farm

Barossa - McClaren Vale - Clare Valley - South Australia
Barich Vineyard, Burge Family (partially), Cape Jaffa Wines, Chapel Hill, Walter Clappis Wine Co., Elderton (partially), Gemtree Vineyards (partially), Hahndorf Hill Winery, Henschke (partially), Hobbs of Barossa Ranges, Kalleske Wines (partially), Kangarilla Road (partially), KT and the Falcon, Lucu Margaux Vineyard, Maverick Wines, Mitchell Winery (partially), Ngeringa, Noon Winery (partially), Paxton Wines, Pertaringa Wines, Radford Wines (partially), Reddenbridge (partially), Sinclair's Gully (partially), Smallfry (partially), Southpaw Vineyard, Tapestry (partially), 919 Wines (partially), Angove Family winemakers (partially), Back Veranda Wines, Battle of Bosworth (partially), Walter Clappis Wine Co., Wirra Wirra (partially), Yangarra (partially)

Heathcote - Yarra Valley – Victoria
All Saints (partially), Amietta (partially), Avonmore Estate, Bass Phillip, Bindi Wine Growers (partially), Bress (partially), Carlei Wines (partially), Castagna Vineyards, Cloudcape

Wines(partially), Cobaw Ridge (partially), Crittenden Wines (partially), Curly Flat (partially), M. Chapoutier (partially), Delatite (partially), Foxey's hangout (partially,), Giant Steps/Innocent Bystander (partially), Goulburn Terrace Wines (partially), Haywards of Locksley, Hockrich, Jasper Hill Wines, Jean Paul's vineyard, King River Estate (partially), Kiltyname Estate, Lethbridge Wines (partially), Limbic Wines, Lloyds Vineyard, Louis de Castella Wines, Moondarra/Holly's Garden, Naked Range (partially), Pennyweight, Prancing Horse, Reese Miller Estate, Robinvale Winery, Roundtable Wines, Savaterre, Shadowfax (partially), Sorrenberg Vineyard, Staindl Wines, Sutton Grange Winery, Tallarook (partially), Tarrington Vineyards, Wedgetail Estate (partially), Wildcroft, Wild Duck Creek

Margaret River - Western Australia
24 Karat, Borrisokane, Burnside Organic Farm, Cowaramup Wines/Clown Fish, Cullen Wines, Gilead Estate, Herriot Wines, Heydon Estate, Hotham Ridge Winery (partially), Howard Park (partially), Jeeleunup Gully, Marri Wood Park, The Lake House, Marchand & Burch, Talijancich Wines (partially), Woody Pear Wines

Tasmania
Brook Eden, Graham Roberts, Moorilla (partially), Stefano Lubiana Wines (partially), Tasmanian Organic Wines (partially), Tony Scherer (partially)

NEW ZEALAND

Blind Trail, Covell Estate, Felton Road, Hawkhurst Estate, Kingsley Estate Vineyards (partially), Millton Vineyards, Pyramid Valley

Vineyards, Rippon, Daniel Schuster Wines (partially), Seresin, Vynfields (partially).

PART 3

O Chateau... the rest of the story.

In case you wondered what happened to OChateau, here's a quick timeline of our crazy adventures:

Quick landmarks:
2004: O Chateau runs its first tastings in a restaurant near the Seine. Not chaotic but close enough.
2005: The Wine Loft! First bottle of Château Margaux opened for a group of Australian clients.
2006: First event organized on the French Riviera... good wine, sunshine: tough. Nicolas joins me to try to turn O Chateau into a real company.
2007: After a fierce selection process (we wore suits), O Chateau is a laureate of the *Paris Entreprendre* group! Prize is ten million euros. No, just kidding on that one. Prize was actually a drunken cocktail party. Works for us.
2008: We set up our fabulous "Champagne Cruise on the Seine river". In May, a client proposes to his girlfriend on one of the cruises. She said... yes!! We're completely broke but we have good stories to tell.
2009: We move into an old wine cellar near the Louvre. After launching Wine Dating evenings for singles in Paris, we get invited to host the first Milanese Wine Dating and make Italy's main news

show (drunk). We wrap up the year organizing somewhere between Paris and Barcelona the Highest Wine Tasting in the World[433].

2010: January 1st 2010: Good resolutions to start drinking less. Jan 6: Really, that was not realistic. We launch successively our *"Grands Crus Tasting"* and our *"Day Trip to Champagne"*. We get written up in The New York Times and in Time Magazine. In November, Olivier releases his first book[434] based on O Chateau's blog. Book becomes a bestseller in a few weeks.

2011: We finally open our brand new home. Fantastic endeavor for us – the place is beautiful: we are beyond broke but excited like never before. Probably because when we conceived the new place, we thought putting a wine bar in the middle of it would be a cool thing to do... We have a Californian chef, making some of the best food in Paris. Gosh we love what we do.

2012: Our Wine Bar is the first Parisian wine bar to ever receive the Wine Spectator Award of Excellence. *Bonjour Paris* ranks us *"Best Wine Bar in Paris"*. We're now a team of 12 lucky ones sharing our wonderful passion for food and wine.

2013: After France, Australia, or Hungary, my wine travel TV show is out in India! The book you're reading comes out after 4 years of work[435]. We're still spending our days spreading the gospel of the good things. And we couldn't be more thankful for it.

Please revert to the last page of this book for a special offer. Ready to join the fun?!

---

[433] By the way, did you know that at 36,000 feet, you get drunk three times faster?
[434] Entitled *Dessine-moi un Parisien* in French and *Stuff Parisians Like* in English. New York magazine calls it "Hilariously perceptive!".
[435] I know: hard to believe!!

RECOMMENDED DOCUMENTARIES

Rather than compiling a dry and incomplete bibliography, I chose to put together a list of good documentaries. If the subjects tackled in this book interest you, the following films are good resources. Good news is: most are available for free online.

This is not an endorsement of what is said in these various films (or how things are presented), but merely an invitation to keep learning and stay inspired.

Food & Wine:

Food Matters
Mondovino
Think Global, Act Rural

Food, Wine and Health industries:

Our Daily Poison
The world according to Monsanto
Burzynski, cancer is serious business
Psychiatrie, profits macabres[436]
Why in the world are they spraying?

---

[436] Rest assured, it's in English- only subtitled in French.

INDEX

A

Alsace, 182, 195
AOC/Appellation, 58, 109, 110, 111, 112, 114, 115, 118, 119, 120
Argentina, 59, 108, 127
Artisanal, 65, 102

B

Bacteria, 33, 35, 36, 178
Biodynamic, 74, 75, 76, 77, 78, 83, 165, 166, 195
Bordeaux, 21, 58, 123, 130, 140, 182, 196
Bourguignon, Claude, 45

C

California, 21, 59, 87, 89, 117, 128
Champagne, 115, 120, 123, 182, 186, 187, 188, 190, 197, 4
Chapoutier, Michel, 19, 77, 199, 208
Chianti, 120
Chile, 59, 108, 127
China, 59, 103
Culture, 22, 25, 29, 59, 65, 87, 100, 103, 104, 117, 119, 143, 145, 155, 167, 168, 171, 4
Cuvée, 109

D

Dirt, 33, 34, 37, 48

F

Farming, 42, 49, 68, 70, 73, 75, 76, 77, 83
Fertilizers, 43, 44, 45, 48, 49, 69
Food, 32, 33, 36, 37, 50, 51, 62, 63, 66, 70, 73, 80, 81, 82, 83, 84, 103, 132, 141, 144, 155, 161, 168, 169, 171

G

Glasses, 9, 10, 17, 149, 150, 161

H

Health, 52, 81, 82, 103, 142, 143, 151, 161, 166, 168, 169

I

Innovations, 89, 91, 94
Irrigation, 89
Italy, 59, 109, 114, 117, 130

L

Label, 4, 58, 73, 103, 106, 107, 109, 115, 116, 120, 124, 143
Languedoc, 115, 130, 182
Loire, 76, 115, 182, 187, 198

M

Mondavi, Robert, 100

N

Napa, 25, 114, 115, 187, 204
Natural, 97
New World, 117
Nutrients, 34, 35, 80

O

Ô Chateau, 3
Oak, 87, 93, 94, 167, 180, 183, 189
Organic, 34, 52, 70, 71, 72, 73, 74, 77, 78, 83, 96, 125, 165, 166

P

Paris, 16, 24, 32, 62, 63, 98, 3
Parker, Robert, 95, 136
Pesticides, 43, 44, 45, 48, 49, 52, 69, 70, 71, 73, 115
Piemonte, 10
Provence, 182, 200

R

Rhône, 19, 182, 199
Roots, 34, 36, 123

S

Soil, 4, 9, 28, 29, 32, 33, 34, 35, 36, 37, 38, 43, 44, 45, 46, 48, 49, 50, 52, 69, 70, 75, 77, 78, 80, 93, 115, 148, 160
South Africa, 59, 108, 178, 193

T

Tannins, 180, 189, 191
Temperature, 51, 151, 186
Terroir, 9, 10, 42, 46, 50, 55, 56, 57, 58, 59, 61, 62, 63, 69, 91, 93, 94, 95, 96, 100, 103, 109, 110, 111, 115, 116, 117, 119, 120, 128, 130, 132, 156, 161, 163, 165, 166, 167, 168, 171, 195
Terroirism, 161
Turkey, 69, 103

V

Varietal, 68, 111, 118, 182, 187
, 57, 76, 102
Vintage, 107, 193

W

Wine Store, 166
Winemaker, 10, 19, 87, 93, 98, 100, 143, 179
Winemaking, 10, 29, 86, 87, 88, 89, 93, 94, 95, 96, 97, 106, 117, 188, 191

Y

Yeasts, 94, 98, 115, 167, 178, 179, 183

ACKNOWLEDGEMENTS

I would like to thank each and every client of O Chateau. Over the years, thanks to your support and enthusiasm, you have helped turn a silly idealistic dream into a reality. For that I am and I will remain infinitely grateful.

This book would never have happened without the admirable patience of my friend and business partner Nicolas Paradis. O Chateau would never be the amazing company it is without his hard work, dedication and skills. Merci.

Special thanks too go to the wonderful staff at O Chateau for working hard everyday on sharing their passion.

Thanks to those in the wine world who have inspired me or taught me so much: Jean-Michel, Michel, Seppi, Elie, Olivier, Pierre-Henri, Marie-Do, François.

My friends – Thomas, Benoît, Gilbert, Baptiste, Jonathan, Cameron, Antoine, Augustin, Guillaume, Elizabeth Dyre Caldwell, Rocco, Ollie, Nicolas, Kirstin, Luca, David, Mymy, Tiffany, Colombe, Marie, Kim, Benjamin, Bertrand, Clare, Colwynn, Sara, Sarah, Deyola, Simon, Alexia, Roberto, the Walcotts, the Hermanns, the McKinneys, the Marrels, the Glenn-Phillips, the Arbues, the Arnauds, the iTV gang, the HB clique, *l'equipaggio della Connie* — thanks for your generosity, support and partnership in crime.

Thank you of course to my family—in France and in the US—for their trust and support. And apologies to my *maman* for making her life so stressful.

Last but not least, thanks to my wife, for her hard work, and for the rest.

ORDERS & CONTACT

Please email Olivier at:

olivier.magny.contact@gmail.com

to order (signed) copies of this book or request more information on the following:

Speaking Engagements
Consulting
Teaching

All comments or questions also welcome!

Cheers!

ABOUT THE AUTHOR

Olivier Magny is a French award-winning sommelier. He's the founder of critically acclaimed Paris wine tasting school and wine bar O Chateau (www.o-chateau.com).

Over the years, Olivier has taught wine to well over 50,000 wine lovers, ranging from novices to professionals. He's also the host of a travel TV show based on wine.

Olivier consults for institutions ranging from Hôtel de Crillon to various universities.

Olivier is also the international best-selling author of *Stuff Parisians Like*, and *Dessine-moi un Parisien*.

Find Olivier online:
www.o-chateau.com
www.OlivierMagny.com
www.MisterWineTasting.com

Find Olivier in Paris:
O Chateau
68, rue Jean-Jacques Rousseau
75001 Paris – France.

O Chateau was rated *Best Wine Bar in Paris*[437]

---

[437] In Bonjour Paris – April 2011.

SPECIAL OFFER

As a token of our appreciation for buying this book, and in a continuous effort to share the culture of good wine and good fun, we are happy to extend a

10% DISCOUNT

on your wine tasting experience at O Chateau

Just visit www.o-chateau.com
and use discount code[438]: INTOWINE75

Merci encore.
And see you soon!

---

[438] Offer valid for purchases made on www.o-chateau.com with discount code INTOWINE75. 10% off applies on all *Wine Tastings* and *Day Trips to Champagne*.

Made in the USA
Charleston, SC
09 February 2013